# About the Author

A. M. AlKhalifa is a graphic designer and photographer based in the Kingdom of Bahrain; someone who is always interested in extensive research to discover more about compelling subjects and matters. Exploring different cultures globally to gain further experience has always been an objective for her. She has specialised in photographing aspects of nature and landscapes, and bird photography. Writing has been considered an expressive solution to spread their influence. *Insights for Creatives* is her first formal project.

# Insights for Creatives

# A.M. AlKhalifa

# Insights for Creatives

Olympia Publishers
*London*

**www.olympiapublishers.com**
OLYMPIA PAPERBACK EDITION

**Copyright © A.M. AlKhalifa 2023**

The right of A.M. AlKhalifa to be identified as author of
this work has been asserted in accordance with sections 77 and 78 of
the Copyright, Designs and Patents Act 1988.



A CIP catalogue record for this title is
available from the British Library.

ISBN: 978-1-80074-900-9



First Published in 2023

Olympia Publishers
Tallis House
2 Tallis Street
London
EC4Y 0AB

Printed in Great Britain

# Dedication

To my parents, thank you for your prayers, sacrifices, support and advice.

# Acknowledgements

Many thanks to my family, your love and support has been immense. Many thanks to everyone who has supported me along this journey. Thank you to every soul who has had an impact on me. A special thank you to everyone at Olympia Publishers for making this a reality.

"Art is still, design surrounds you."

–    A. M. AlKhalifa

# Contents

# Introduction

Designers as creative individuals have been the force behind visual communication. Without creative individuals, such an approach would not be as effective as it is known to be. Today, perceivers consider visual communication to be a reliable asset, and most would not be able to function every day of their lives without its presence. Designers literally generate creative thoughts and ideas to develop suitable solutions which basically deliver visual communication. Such creative thoughts and ideas are implemented during a design process with design fundamentals every skilled designer is aware of. In order to develop effective results, creatives should express knowledge and understanding to achieve influential outcomes. Becoming a successful creative requires a vigorous amount of effort and determination, which forces designers to come up with successful and effective solutions constantly. By continuously refreshing creative minds with knowledgeable facts and information, designers gradually gain even further awareness of various surroundings.

Creatives who possess a great amount of knowledge will always be ahead of other individuals whether related to the design industry or not. Experience gives individuals greater knowledge that will always act like an accessible source or reference because of being achieved by oneself. Also, experience plays a major role in self-confidence and personal characteristics, which designers need to develop over time in order to act like professionals. An industry-like design demands for competent creatives who are well aware of the responsibility being faced. Having the ability, knowledge, and skill to excel at an industry like design will be extremely vital for creatives who wish to succeed at such a profession. Surely visual communication has always been seen as a challenging approach, though by expressing proficient skills and abilities, creatives will be well prepared to face any demanding task.

As an approach, visual communication has been the connection between information and perceivers; basically, anyone perceiving communication visually depends on effective solutions produced by creatives. A matter of such significance gives creatives a greater responsibility to achieve successful outcomes, which, without an approach like visual communication, would totally end up being ineffective towards a desired target. Achieving pleasing results which are effective at the same time gives designers an opportunity to be in control of spreading a communicative message which is being visually transmitted. An approach like visual communication will continue to be a significant way to deliver information. For graphic designers especially, the responsibility being faced will always be substantial, since outcomes from such a profession should always be influential in order to be effective.

Graphic design has evolved immensely over the years, though the purpose has always been the same ever since the beginning of its emergence during the fifteenth century. In 1922, the term 'Graphic Designer' officially emerged, when American designer William Addison Dwiggins referred to it as his own profession. Dwiggins was widely known as a commercial designer previously, since most of his work included typography and book design. Though even after affirming such a term, graphic design was only widely known and used after the Second World War. However, the credit still belongs to Dwiggins, since the term originally appeared in America. Graphic designers today should be aware of the founder behind a term like 'Graphic Design', because a title discovered by a fellow creative was the cause for such a term to be widely recognised and globally known.

Today, many individuals consider graphic design as more than just a creative profession. Ever since an approach of such prominence was introduced to the public, the one and only purpose was to be able to spread visual communication in a persuasive manner. Influencing perceivers requires more than just particular skills; understanding is a key factor in order to develop such effective solutions, which is why a profession like graphic design is regarded as a diverse profession compared to other design branches, since science and creativity merge with one another to form effective solutions. Creatives who are not aware of the importance of influencing others through visual means will not be able to develop successful outcomes. Most creatives today also refer to graphic design as visual communication depending on certain results and outcomes being developed at a certain time. Since the primary principle of graphic design is executing visual communication through creative aspects, as a profession, graphic design could also be known as visual communication or effective communication.

Since the purpose of such a discipline deals with more than just creativity, the development of visually communicative results should actually impact others as well, which requires complete concentration while processing influential results that have to be effective towards an intended target. Supporting an outcome with research and inspiration gives creatives a broader understanding whenever dealing with a development process. Therefore, creative individuals should always gain further knowledge and keep looking for inspiration that could affect a creative outcome. Only with enough support will creatives find a suitable solution that somehow impacts others while being effective at the same time. Achieving such persuasive results will lead designers to greater challenges which deals with even greater impact. Challenges of such worth will continue to supply creatives with even further experience, which will transform individual abilities to a much more capable level.

Creative individuals should always aim to achieve results that impact others in order to be successful at accomplishing the objectives such a profession demands. While developing creative solutions, designers should be completely aware of the purpose behind an expected solution to develop outcomes based on certain needs. 'Insights for Creatives' is meant to inspire individuals and creatives to become more influential towards perceivers. Design is more than just an ordinary profession; creatives should realise that creative solutions are meant to influence others while conveying certain messages. Exploring what other creatives have achieved over time gradually inspires others to become even more inventive. Enlightening one's understanding by reading insights from other creatives expands and broadens knowledge of a creative possesses while gaining useful facts and information.

As a whole, 'Insights for Creatives' is divided into multiple chapters which are based on matters related to graphic design and visual communication. Also, topics included are identified as in-depth discussions based on personal views and opinions which have been supported by extended research. Discussing matters related to the creative industry based on experience gives readers the chance to recognise unfamiliar subjects and facts. Such thoughtful expressions are meant to inspire readers to become more creative while raising awareness levels. Topics stated mainly refer to the creative industry, which is widely known to be an influential field where creativity collides with science to have a desired effect on perceivers. Chapters in this book are divided based on history, fundamentals, and practice concerning the creative industry. It is vital for designers to be aware of the basics before beginning to develop further skills, since a solid foundation will greatly support the development of creative ideas while raising experience levels too.

Generally, influential material such as insights may inspire any individual at any time. Any of the content involved in this book would not necessarily be intended for individuals who have a creative background, though any individual who has the desire to feel enlightened might be affected in a way, or even encouraged to pursue a career in design as well. 'Insights for Creatives' may also be referred to whenever in doubt or facing a complicated situation, since thoughtful words which have been expressed in an influential way may seem to be the answer to solving unexpected creative conflicts that might be faced. As creative individuals, designers should be proficient individuals who express knowledgeable skills and understanding. Looking for informative sources which are inspiring will be necessary for any improvement or development to be noticed in skills.

Designers should keep enhancing knowledgeable attributes in order to maintain creativity. Gaining useful facts, information, and becoming aware of various subjects will give creatives the opportunity to develop thinking abilities. Surely developing personal characteristics and attributes constantly will be vital for creatives who wish to succeed. An industry such as the creative industry always demands for general enhancement in order to enable creative thinking, which without, an industry of such significance would result as ineffective. Continuing to activate features which leads to creative thinking helps designers generate ideas more frequently. Any source which leads creatives to implementing imaginative thinking abilities becomes known as a reliable reference. Whether creatives find such influential sources from words, facts, or thoughts does not matter, as long as outcomes continue to impact others. After all, each individual becomes totally in control of their own decisions, which causes intentions to gradually unfold.

An approach like visual communication will always request creative individuals with certain abilities. Creatives who produce outcomes that influence perceivers while transmitting a desired message. Designers who continue developing individual characteristics will succeed at a profession of such significance. Intentionally, the reason to create and develop such influential results is to spread awareness as perception becomes affected. Portraying any sort of communication through visual means requires skills and understanding. As creative individuals, designers should seek knowledgeable facts and information in order to reinforce decisions yet to be made in such a challenging industry. In a field like design, opinions matter greatly, since judging during a design process or evaluating a specific outcome requires individuals who are totally aware of the purpose of visual communication. Experience will be a key factor during such times, since anything creatives gain logically will result to be insightful or intuitive. Creatives who keep enhancing individual characteristics will be confident whenever taking the lead.

It is with experience that designers gradually develop professional skills. Especially for creatives, professionalism and competence will be necessary in order to generate a successful creative system. Creatives who possess a proficient way of thinking gradually become individuals with distinctive capabilities. Also, the quality of outcomes being developed by such experienced creatives becomes easily noticed because of the amount of thought expressed. Nowadays, an approach like visual communication is recognised globally because of perceivers and consumers who force such an approach to become effective. Relying on such an effective approach makes it possible for creatives to experiment and develop creative ideas which are entirely intended to have an impact. Controlling a design process to achieve such influential results leads to even further effective solutions that communities, societies, and people depend on to function typically. Allowing visual communication to direct and control actions and behaviour shows how substantial such an approach continues to be. By realizing the significance behind such visually attractive results, designers become encouraged promptly to develop effective solutions repeatedly.

Surely no one can ever deny the fact that visual communication has evolved tremendously over the years. Designers certainly deserve to be acknowledged and appreciated for developing an approach like visual communication. It is with desire and determination from creatives of the past and present that has caused graphic design to be recognised remarkably. Creatives of the future should also continue the path to impress perceivers by producing imaginative solutions. Graphic design as a profession will continue to impact perceivers globally as long as creatives keep generating creative ideas that are influential yet persuasive. Enlightening one's soul with beneficial information causes ideas and thoughts to unfold. Basically, creatives will not be able to generate creative thinking without such influential material. Creatives should seek to become inquisitive individuals in order for such a profession to flourish further. Such attempts from designers will greatly affect outcomes that cause visual communication to thrive in a positive way.

# Chapter 1
## About Graphic Design

Thinking of communication makes you realise how important design is or was. Nowadays, people refer to Graphic Design as Visual Communication because of the importance design plays in our everyday lives. Design is a way of creative thinking, it's a way of life, and, most importantly, it solves communicative problems.

People are exposed to design every day of their lives; they are surrounded by it and consume it on a daily basis. Not many people realise this or even appreciate the hard work designers express to produce such things. From packaged foods for breakfast to the signs on the road that lead you to places, advertisements that makes you want things, books that spread knowledge, digital devices that help you communicate with family and friends; it's all in there; design is all around us, but who pays attention to such things? What would people do if their foods didn't have labels, or if the roads were plain and without signs? It is important to understand that visual communication leads you visually to places, things, objects, etc. It is important because it matters greatly to consumers that need designers to think creatively and solve problems.

Design is a vigorously changing field, going back to the fifteenth century when type and letterforms were first introduced, to the evolution of design which began during the nineteenth century when the Arts and Crafts movement began.

Movements of such began to influence creatives to be productive and therefore inspire generations to come. This led to different movements and styles being introduced. The Arts and Crafts movement was the first movement of all, being mainly a movement that focused on decorative arts and architecture. Art Nouveau followed soon after; a style which was known for natural and floral forms. Inspired by flowers and plants, Art Nouveau mainly influenced graphics, fashion, and consumer products. De Stijl, a Dutch art movement which translated to 'the style', was a truly new style that began during the early twentieth century which attracted designers, artists, and architects. De Stijl was a style that was so effective because the styles were committed to uniting the varieties of art into one style.

Another major inspiring movement was the Bauhaus, based in Germany during the early twentieth century. Bauhaus was a school dedicated strictly to design. Walter Gropius was the founder of the school whose styles kept influencing generations of designers and still does to this day. This was all due to the newly introduced ideas that the community went along with. There are many other styles that kept influencing creatives throughout the twentieth century, even though both World Wars had affected some styles and movements along the way.

Each and every style and movement had greatly affected designers to produce and create designs that were up to date at a specific period of time. However, certain styles and movements didn't continue to evolve much during the twenty first century. Everything people see now is post modernism, which is all based on influences from the past. Influences that continue to inspire designers and leave a mark on current productions because of all the styles and movements acting like a strong and vital foundation to kick-start anything.

Successful designers always begin with a strong base. The first thing designers should always do before beginning their design process is to research wisely. By researching, designers will be able to gain more knowledge in order to back up their intentions and initial ideas. Whether it be branding, packaging, or an environmental design, having researched about particular topics, cultures, and styles eases the process for designers to begin generating ideas in order to build a concept.

Researching is one of the main principles of design. There are many ways to research; it's not just about scrolling through different artworks and previous designs to get inspired to do something that is similar. It is more like a way of understanding and comprehending the subject. Creatives must think of researching as a short task, an investigation, and a way of exploration that would lead to numerous inspirations and ideas. That way, building a concept for any intended design would become easier to construct. On the other hand, researching can also act like a useful backing towards the end of any design process and while presenting expected design developments to clients or colleagues.

Another major principle of design is composition, which is all about visual structure and the arrangement of various elements within a design. Composition is all about organizing and putting together the design as a whole, complete piece before starting to design the actual concept. Different layouts and grids are explored and tested by designers before beginning a creative process, in order to achieve the suited layout for any design. It is all about perceiving the whole design instead of dividing each element separately. Basically, composition is just as important as the elements that make up a design like text, image, and colour. Understanding form and space helps designers to come up with attractive and appealing layouts. When it comes to composition the graphic eye and how elements are implemented are extremely crucial towards outcomes. Professionals and creatives can judge any design based on what they see. It could either be positive or negative feedback; it all comes down to the visual talent they have. The graphic eye is a somewhat natural matter where talented people have the eyes to spot graphic details in everything they see. More importantly, it's the years of practice, knowledge, and creative thinking which develops individuals into professionals.

Brainstorming is a key factor for creatives to come up with new ideas and establish new forms that would be useful while creating grids and layouts that form the overall design. There are different ways of brainstorming; the key purpose of doing so opens up the mind to gradually develop creative and inspiring ideas. To master the perfect composition, designers must think of how to fill any blank space to create form, balance, and movement. Layouts of designs could be symmetrical or asymmetrical; it all relies on a designer's point of view and how designers see it to be, just like visualizing intentions of a creative idea and layout possibilities. Designers get the chance to be creative by exploring different aspects of design. Flexibility is the right word to describe any designer who is in the process of creating and problem solving. Creative individuals who explore various layouts during an expected design process will be able to achieve innovative styles that assist an overall design. Mainly, the result of a successful and creative composition shows towards the end of the design production. Audiences could either applaud or criticise designs, but, either way, designers should accept any judgement whether it be good or bad, so that designers can learn and gain experience to be successful in the future.

Typography is considered to be a crucial principle of design. We are surrounded by it; typography is everything that communicates with us visually. The process of arranging letters, words, and text is what typography is all about. Every context the human eye observes communicates in its own way. There is a language in between that transmits communication directly. All the different languages we observe today have their own way of communication. Basically, the formation of letters that form words which communicate visually in any specific language is what typography is all about. Most importantly, typography is a combination of art and science. For creatives, it's always important to keep this core combination in mind in order to create and produce outcomes and solutions that remain in connection with the rules and guidelines of typography.

When it comes to colour, which is the fourth principle of design, creatives must fully understand how to choose and assign colours for any intended project. Colour selections can be tricky at times, therefore understanding a principle of such is completely essential for designers. Also, it is important to keep in mind that colour could affect legibility in any form. While selecting and choosing a specific colour scheme for a design, creatives should always consider harmony and contrast whenever making decisions. Issues like these can help ease any decisions designers make.

Also, it's vital to keep in mind that printed inks are different from screen-based colours. When it comes to the printing process, there will always be a system that printers use in order to have a smooth process. During printing, colour is processed automatically. Ink distribution is based on four major colours that all printers use, which also makes up and forms other colours during printing. This identification is known as 'CMYK', which is broken down to cyan, magenta, yellow, and black. These colours are what printers use for print-making today. Although colours seen on screen are different to the colours used for print making, additive primaries and RGB light create the colours seen on screens like computers, television, and monitors. Additive colours are known as RGB, which stands for red, green, and blue. When the system is combined and active, white light is generated to support the appearance since such a colour system is used for screen purposes only.

Colours are somewhat regarded as influential in a way that attracts perception based on individual preferences. History, culture, memory, experience, and intelligence all play a part in colour perception. It is more like psychology and its relation to emotional response. Understanding colour well enough gives the advantage of knowing how it is considered to be emotional and that it is more like a language which interacts with different cultures around the world. Colour is also very effective in a psychological sense. When it comes to organizing components of any project, designers should be aware that any colour palette they select for their designs will have an immediate effect on the audience or consumers. As a result, the first thing that attracts audiences and consumers is colour, especially when it comes to selections. Psychologists have proven in many studies that humans get attracted to any object by its colour before its content.

Overall, colour is a very vital principle of design. It is considered to be effective in many ways which makes it a tough task for designers to decide on. Selecting colours for specific designs requires creatives who understand carefully who their target group is. Also selecting certain colour schemes that best suits each project will greatly be helpful towards the final outcome. Colour is so powerful in many ways; it can be perceived in a positive or negative way, which makes it necessary for designers to carefully study the process of decision-making before implementing anything into their designs. Combining the four principles of design leads to successful outcome all the time. Designers must learn to merge and combine the four principles in order to accomplish and fulfil creative thinking. It is important to keep in mind that creative thinking doesn't happen all of a sudden. There will always be a cause that leads the designer to a creative thought. Being imaginative is also another way to process creativity. By being imaginative, designers become able to visualise new aspects that make up the initial design. It is more like having the chance to see unconventional ideas. Imagination leads to fresh features and characteristics which build up an idea and take it to a totally new level. Just like a useful tool, imagination could be convenient for aspiring designers of all levels.

Creative thinking is what designers nowadays need to focus on. Learning doesn't just stop after college. A successful designer should always seek to learn new aspects about the creative world. That way, creatives will be able to generate new ideas our community needs. It is very vital that creatives show and express their passion towards what they intend to do. Without passion and desire, creatives would not be able to build on their base. Being passionate is like expressing willingness and affection towards one's profession. In order to flourish as an individual in the creative industry, creatives must show passion towards their profession, practice more regularly, and always be persistent.

Our world today requires designers and creatives who act like leaders have a voice of their own. To become a leader that leads by example, one must apply leadership skills into their roles. A career hierarchy would state that creative directors and art directors would act like leaders or bosses. Then comes the designers who are split into two titles (Senior Designers and Junior Designers). Third comes the developers such as the brand developer and content developer.

Looking at the career hierarchy would reveal that there is only one leader running the design agency or firm, and possibly a second leader who would act like a vice leader. Everyone else would just be regarded as finishers and implementers. It is very rare to come across a leader who is true to themselves, unfortunately. Someone who is passionate about what they do. Sadly, our community today lacks these types of characters. We are certainly in need of fresh personalities nowadays. Creative directors must indeed be more aware of their surroundings. Directors who act like true leaders instead of being more dependent and relying on other individuals that take part in multiple jobs all at once. A leader in the design world should always act like a reliable person, someone who has a fresh voice and to always be a dependable individual. If all creative directors care about their profession and act like proper leaders, surely the design industry will always move forward, producing creative innovations. Our community is definitely in need of creative problem solvers who are willing to generate and produce visual solutions.

Overall, graphic design is a field where graphic designers will always seek to learn in order to improve their knowledge and understanding even further. Designers, as creatives, have the ability to develop their individual skills to become more productive. It's important for designers to always feel the need to produce creative solutions that our community and world needs. Whether it's for a good cause, or even an awareness movement, everything can be worthy. Combining function and aesthetics together will produce designers who are able to generate creative thoughts that are valuable for our industry. To make it sound simple, function is somewhat like a cause or a specific design that is developed by a designer, whereas aesthetics is more like subjectivity in a specific design, when an artist or designer becomes more influential in what they intend on producing.

Designers nowadays should take on independent decisions to try and learn from their mistakes. Being dependent on someone else and always trying to be reliable will result in inactivity, or more so slothful characteristics. Art directors nowadays should be inspiring younger generations by engaging them with the process of design. In order to have an active environment, one must hope to aspire, always be ambitious, and to continually hope to achieve their best. Our design industry today is in need of influential mentors who are always willing to inspire the younger generation to produce their utmost best. Always trying to impress someone is the proper character a designer should have. Nonetheless. every designer or creative should have great passion to strive for more.

# Chapter 2
## Style in Graphic Design

Most probably a term used by all designers while presenting is 'style'. It is a matter of concern for some creatives as well, especially during the beginning of their design process. Designers as individuals should think of style as a set of creative thoughts that helps build an idea of whatever they intend on producing. Style is a term used very often in the design industry, because it's all about the inspirations and creativity that leads any designer into producing innovative ideas.

There are two aspects of style; the first aspect of style would be when a designer is using an existing style or a style that has already existed for a specific period of time. In that case, it is considered as an inspiration or an influence from something that has or will help a designer to produce and design literally anything depending on their actual intentions. The second aspect of style is considered to be an individual matter, more like a personal style or an approach that defines a designer's character, or like when a designer becomes regarded by others for their creative techniques and productions. In that case, a designer becomes known for their specific style which is implemented throughout whatever they seek to produce and create. Designers in general are known to be creative individuals who have the power to change people's thoughts. For graphic designers specifically, style is considered to be a vital aspect for any creative process.

Knowing which style inspires a creative individual, or gradually building ideas that generate into a specific style, will result in the creative innovation our industry strives for. It is very vital for graphic designers to specify a style that best suits their approach while intending to design for any purpose. Only then will it be easier for designers to generate their creative abilities and produce creative work. Being aware of a style that best suits a designer for a specific project will open up all the creative doors so that designers can accomplish their task without complications, though a designer should always bear in mind that using the same style for consecutive projects will result in replication, which will lead to boring results.

For instance, a designer is handed a brief that requires a poster design for an awareness campaign. The designer then goes for a typographic-inspired style, which ends up being successful. However, a couple of weeks later another brief is received; this time, though, the designer is asked to design a packaging line for a tea brand. Should the designer stick to the same style they got applauded for? Or should they go for a new approach which might feel risky at some stage? If you are thinking that sticking to the same style will lead you to more success, that would be inappropriate surely because designers should always have a confident character that is not afraid to take any risks. Feeling assured and showing confidence will lead to an optimism, such characteristics that designers should always try to attempt; without being optimistic, designers will lose the confidence and positivity they will need evermore.

The graphic design industry has been through an enormous transformation of styles throughout the past, which lead to a significant base for present and future designers to prosper.

Styles and movements of the past will always act as an inspiration to existing designers.

Although some movements lasted for a short period of time, they will always be as effective as the rest. Not only will past styles and movements act as an inspiration and influence designers, but such impactful approaches will also become the foundation of any project designers intend on working on.

Ever since the late nineteenth century, when the first creative movement was established during exciting times, the design industry flourished and grew to become more inventive and imaginative to keep inspiring generations to come, beginning with the Arts and Crafts movement (1880–1910), a movement which focused solely on decorative and fine arts. One of the notable icons of that period of time was British textile designer William Morris. Art Nouveau (1890–1915) was another international style which inspired designers and artists alike; a style that was inspired by curves of nature like plants and flowers. Austrian symbolist painter and artist Gustav Klimt was notable for that style.

Another major style which began in the early twentieth century was Art Deco (1925–1940); an architectural style with influences from visual arts and design. Art Deco implementations began in France before the First World War. Mainly Art Deco influenced buildings, jewellery, and cars. However, visual artists and designers find this style as inspiring as any because of how shapes are very precisely structured. Also, another major design movement which inspired Europe mainly was De Stijl, which is Dutch for 'The Style'. The movement flourished from (1920–1930), and mainly consisted of artist and architects. Geometric layouts and straight lines were a stand-out during the movement. Designers today can benefit a lot from a movement like De Stijl, because of how aligned and structured layouts played a major role at a time when designers were just beginning to develop. These are just some of the notable styles and movements that continue to influence designers today. Not only because such movements and styles transformed the design industry, but because such periods are considered to be the foundation of our creative industry which will continue to inspire future designers as part of history.

After the Second World War, designers began to think of new approaches that could help an industry like design to revive itself. During the war, designers and creative individuals were not very active, societies were disturbed, and people of all sorts were literally traumatised. To help the industry revitalise, creative minds needed to get closer and have an impact on societies to make them feel somewhat rejuvenated. What better way to help connect with societies than with visual communication? One significant way which led designers to become more active was poster design. Posters were designed to keep people informed; even soldiers during the war received flyers to keep them well informed about what was going on. It is still considered to be one of the easiest ways to spread communicative messages, because all the important information stands out on one page. Design agencies nowadays also design posters for branding purposes. It shows how a field like visual communication can not only be about creative communication, but a beneficial and worthy process at the same time.

The international typographic style began to evolve right after the Second World War, and so designers became aware of the importance of typography. Therefore, new approaches were introduced during that period of time; mainly the international typographic style was developed during the 1950s in Switzerland. Even though the style existed in other European countries like Germany, Russia, and the Netherlands before the Second World War, it didn't have as much influence on the public as much as when the style evolved after the war in Switzerland.

Akzidenz-Grotesk was a sans serif typeface that was used commonly for printing purposes across Europe – mainly Germany, though. Everything about this typeface speaks to modernism, which led to satisfaction from users. Also, Akzidenz-Grotesk was what influenced Swiss designers to create typefaces with similar characteristics. Legibility, simplicity, and innovation are the main features of Swiss-style designs. One of the main standouts of the international typographic style was Helvetica, a sans serif typeface created by Max Miedinger and Eduard Hoffmann; the typeface was developed during 1957. It was a typeface that became so popular worldwide, not because of how effective it was, but because it was so legible that it could be used anywhere for any purpose. Basically, it was and still is to this day considered as the all-in-one typeface, not just because it was executed professionally, but because Helvetica is a typeface that pleases the eyes whenever perceived.

Designers during the 1950s began focusing on making typography stand out to the public. You could notice from artworks during the Swiss style how designers had clear visions of very well-structured layouts and creative typographic instalments. Uses of asymmetric layouts and sans serif typefaces were frequent during the Swiss style. The design industry needed something new at a time when creative minds were still recovering. So, when the international typographic style or Swiss style evolved, it felt like the design industry as a whole reinvigorated itself. Everything about the Swiss style speaks contemporary; it was indeed the style that transformed creative individuals at that time. It is still considered to be a crucial style today for designers and creative minds who are always on the lookout for inspirations.

Nowadays, graphic designers have enough knowledge and information that could be useful in solving any design problem. A foundation that has been evolving for centuries with new movements in style has led to a strong base for current and future designers to always look out for. It is important for designers as individuals to always learn from the past, making sure that styles and developments of the past will continue to inspire designers of the future one way or another. Seeking to learn will be beneficial for designers at some stage of their careers; everyone needs facts and information to boost their thinking. By having an in depth understanding, designers begin to develop their skills by interpreting previous movements and styles of the design industry in order to gradually produce a style of their own. By combining thoughts, creatives will also be able to generate ideas to create a personal style that reflects their characters. Designers could consider previous styles as inspirations.

But what if styles of the past got recognised as educational material? Wouldn't that change how designers as individuals think? Instead of just looking for inspiration, creatives could research in depth about a creative field such as graphic design, so that designers become more enlightened and aware about specific subjects in detail. A graphic designer's job requires around fifty per cent of thinking and fifty per cent of executing. Creatives think to design, think to produce, and always think of the outcome. But has anyone wondered how? It all comes down to one's research and how much effort has been put into it.

Without being aware of your discipline, you won't be able to succeed at your practice. Awareness is all about having the knowledge of what you do and becoming an individual who looks for information to progress and develop individual skills. Being well aware of your profession will make you ingenious. Creatives should always thrive to become individuals who are resourceful yet inventive at the same time; individuals who are able to overcome obstacles in order to be innovative. With such characteristics, creatives will evolve into professional individuals who get to reveal their passion.

# Chapter 3
## Solving a Design Problem

Part of your profession as a graphic designer is problem solving. So, to begin and solve any problem you receive, you will have to be efficient before the design process. It is crucial to keep in mind that a design problem is more like a cause which leads the designer to begin any design process. More like a source that is informative yet still requiring a solution. Every design problem has to be solved, though it is down to a designer's cleverness and proficiency to react in an appropriate way. Either working with a team or individually, designers should demonstrate their intelligence by always interpreting the fundamentals of design throughout the design process. Researching well enough about the design problem will be useful and very helpful while designing. Being well informed about any subject will enlighten designers to generate creative thoughts and strengthen their capabilities in problem solving. Designers as individuals have the ability to produce and generate ideas in order to solve problems related to design while incorporating creativity at the same time.

Upon receiving a design brief, designers are asked to come up with a solution and produce creative material to satisfy their client. Some designers may succeed yet others might fail. It all relies on that first impression a designer thought of and how they have managed to respond to it. Solving a design problem requires intense understanding right from the beginning. By understanding a particular design brief, designers become aware of the problem they are about to solve. So, each creative individual gradually begins to build their thinking around their intentions. Once designers have identified the purpose of a design brief the solving phase then begins to emerge. This next step enables creative thinking as designers begin to generate imaginative thoughts and ideas. As creatives, designers are able to accumulate their creative thoughts to produce solutions that are visually communicative. Also, as individuals, graphic designers should always have the eagerness to produce a creative solution. Without enthusiasm, creative individuals will lack inventiveness and become more indolent. Having a keen character will lead creatives to innovation and being imaginative at the same time.

Design thinking is mainly part of the design process, more like a phase every designer goes through in order to produce and generate creative thoughts. Part of design thinking requires imagination; by being imaginative, designers will be able to form new creative ideas which will act as a strong foundation to any design process. Imagination should also be considered by designers as a key to creativity. Having a vivid image of the actual design or the final solution will help designers develop creative ideas regularly with ease. Developing ideas will then lead to productivity, and gradually the design process begins to unfold. Focusing on the design problem throughout the thinking process will also lead to an innovative outcome.

The second part of design thinking is inspiration. Creative individuals will be able to develop their imaginative thoughts and ideas once they have been inspired by their surroundings. Inspiration is what designers should attempt to find before any design process takes place. This is all because of the great impact an inspiration has on the final design. Basically, inspirations act like influences which are effective and efficacious. Creative individuals should think of inspirations as sources yet to be found, sources which are hidden everywhere still waiting to be seen. From objects to thoughts to movements, a particular source that could have an immediate effect on creatives. It is much easier to think of an inspiration as a source which evolves to affect designers in some way or another, so that they are able to create and be inventive at the same time. Combining imaginations with inspirations will benefit designers greatly by helping them generate creative ideas during both the thinking and design process in a productive manner.

Another essential aspect of solving a design problem is having a strategy before any design process begins. Assembling a strategy will help creative individuals achieve their aim. Having a plan ready before beginning the actual design process will not only benefit designers in achieving their intentions. Designers will also get to be more organised throughout the design process which will also help designers get to their deadlines on time to satisfy their clients.

Creative individuals should always act like professionals during their practice. By being a creative professional, designers will be more successful in their careers. In order for that success to flourish, creatives must always have a strategy that leads them to accomplish their intentions while also attaining certain objectives set prior to the design process. The main goal of having a strategy is helping guide creatives throughout their design process. Whether creatives are strategizing individually or as a group, it is vital to keep in mind that the purpose of any strategy is to come up with a solution that solves a specific design problem. Once a strategy has been set and planned by either a design team or an individual, it will be time for creatives to move on to the second phase of the process which is structure. During this phase, designers have to be able to combine the elements of design in order to produce and create whatever they have planned for during the previous phase.

Developing those creative ideas will lead designers gradually into the design process. During the design process designers should always try and develop their designs further down the line in order to get to the final solution. Developing a specific design is like adding and adjusting different aspects of the initial design. During this process, creatives will be able to experiment with their ideas and feel free to gradually develop them before it's too late to make any adjustments. At the same time, this phase of development will surely be beneficial for designers and creatives alike. Designers will benefit greatly while applying specific skills since such an experience will be rewarding towards creative individuals as knowledgeable attributes are gained. Moments like these help creatives to naturally develop confidence. A confident designer is someone who is aware of their abilities; a self-assured character who is always able to lead with example. Creatives nowadays should build their confidence by practicing more often, learning from their mistakes to strengthen their belief in their capabilities. The structure process is about being able to implement creative ideas to produce a visual yet communicative answer that reflects to what was planned ahead.

Assuring that the process ends up a success, creative individuals must have a system that links up a strategy to a structure plan. A successful system requires bonding different phases to produce a solution for a design problem. Connecting from phase to phase makes it easier for designers to understand a design problem more clearly. From strategizing to planning, to analysing, designing, and implementing, designers should go through certain phases carefully to achieve a productive system that supports and fulfils their intentions. Linking together specific phases will also help creative individuals understand a design process distinctly. Making sure that a system flows steadily without complications is important for creatives. Avoiding obstacles throughout the process will help balance any active system as well. After all, meeting deadlines is also part of a successful system. Ensuring that all deadlines are met on time will be vital for designers to keep track of their schedule during the design process. To achieve goals and intentions previously set, creatives must set deadlines in a specific period of time to help individuals overcome any obstacles. At the same time, creatives will have enough time to assess their progress each time a deadline is set throughout the implementation process.

Evaluating a design can be tricky at times, especially if designers are producing individual work. By evaluating, designers become more like judges, giving opinions and views based on their own knowledge. Assessment should be a fun process, like motivating designers to speak of what they know and give their honest opinions. Being assessed however can be frightening at times, especially if you're a design student presenting your work to your professor. Or even whenever a junior designer would be presenting ideas and mock-ups to a creative director. Either way, designers should accept any feedback given in order to be able to adjust and modify whatever suggested by professionals because their experience matters greatly and effectively. Knowing that your work did not meet expected standards during a certain period of time can be really harsh. Affected feelings can have a definite impact on a designer's personality which could result in affecting their designs. Avoiding these harsh comments will be useful during assessments, a phase filled with advice, guidance, and directions is what an assessment should always look like. After all, every individual loves a bit of praise. To hear those words of appreciation and admiration will surely cheer those creative souls. Encouragement without a doubt strengthens an individual's mentality. Therefore, supporting creative individuals will boost their confidence to continue producing creative yet effective results. Professionals from the creative industry should act like motivational leaders, who tend to influence designers and creatives all the time to become productive and innovative. A cheerful atmosphere will spread optimism amongst creative individuals; confidence will soon follow and so a productive system is commenced.

Creative individuals should embrace creativity while solving a design problem. By thinking creatively, designers will be able to generate ideas more frequently. Imaginative ideas will lead designers to successful solutions. The final result will demonstrate and reveal how inventive the designer was. It is extremely vital that designers include their voice throughout the design process. The voice of a creative individual expresses their identity whenever producing creative solutions. A creative identity is more like an independent character who reveals their influences towards the outcome. Adding individual touches to a specific design could be expressed as the voice of the designer.

Experience also plays a major role in having a voice; the knowledge gained and skills obtained differs from one individual to another. Experienced designers will have an advantage because of their knowledge. All that collaboration in the design field will act in favour of a creative individual's character and somehow be beneficial when it comes to being decisive. Interacting with one another will help spread all that experience and knowledge shared amongst designers. Creatives will be involved in discussions that matter tremendously.

Confidence will then follow, and gradually individuals will be able to shape their voice. Reaching a point where individuals feel confident in themselves will help creatives evolve into mature individuals. That self-belief will indeed be useful yet exceptional at the same time. Maintaining that confidence will certainly be difficult; after all, designers are human beings. Distancing yourself from that emotional factor will help preserve confidence in a character. Becoming aware of a specific design problem and fully understanding the conflict which needs to be solved makes it uncomplicated for creative individuals to sustain their confidence.

In a way, a design problem could be compared to a challenging task, or more like a mission only an eager designer should face. Demonstrating that willingness and desire will help creatives achieve successful results. Challenging individual abilities will also assist designers with their performance. By accepting specific challenges and overcoming any obstacles, creatives will be able to achieve their intentions yet also manage to find a solution at the same time. Creative individuals should never underestimate their capabilities. As individuals, designers are trained to face visual communication problems, though to be successful in solving certain problems, designers must display determination. Eagerness and willingness are also characteristics designers should unveil during any expected design process. With such indispensable characteristics, designers will be able to fulfil their objectives while embracing creativity at the same time.

# Chapter 4
## The Unconventional Designer

Creative thinkers today should consider featuring new methods that are yet to be tested in the field. Conventional thinking is based upon general and common ideas of our design industry. Consumers are getting used to replication and reproduction, therefore existing ideas are beginning to affect designers and their creativeness. As creatives, designers should always have the desire to be innovative and produce unpredictable designs.

A typical designer is someone who is unnoticed, lost amongst other designers. Someone who produces a standard level of quality, with no intention of challenging their abilities. Typical designers could also be described as content individuals who are accepting at the same time. This feeling of satisfaction could destroy the act of creativity and the ability to generate inventive ideas. However, by thinking unconventionally, creatives will be able to free themselves from any barriers and somehow be conspicuous. Our design industry today doesn't need individuals with conventional characteristics who only base their designs on existing and common ideas that have not been well thought of. Though creative individuals should pursue innovation and attempt to feature new methods at the same time, by introducing original ideas that are true to oneself, individuals will be able to achieve unconventional thinking.

Common ideas are based upon existing designs from the past. If designers limit themselves from testing risky ideas, they will never be able to witness their capabilities. Therefore, thinking outside the box is a must for creative individuals who are willing to pursue innovation.

Designs which are common amongst consumers are basically general ideas that have been produced and developed. But what if designers developed those ideas further down the line? Basic ideas would then evolve into fresh yet inventive ideas. Creatives are mistaken to have thought that a first or an initial idea could not be developed any further. Normally, this is a common mistake designers go through during their design process. Thinking that your basic idea will lead you throughout the design process will result in an incomplete design that lacks creativity and looks partially finished. Developing basic ideas further down the line will help designers realise the importance of the design process. Where mistakes are acceptable and adjustments are appreciated, any basic idea would have by then developed into a successful solution a designer was after.

Thinking conventionally could also limit designers from progressing and growing as individuals. Referring to traditional methods will limit designers from generating imaginative ideas, going for conventional styles whenever designing will lead designers to results that are common instead of inventive. Creative individuals should prevent themselves from any limitations that could affect their overall performance. Whether designing a typeface or coming up for a solution, creatives should always attempt to find ways of their own and try to define their original character. Keeping a distance from conventional styles and methods will not only benefit designers as individuals, but continuing this phase with determination, and keeping a distance from conventional styles, will help designers introduce new, innovative ways of problem solving. A designer is someone who should express their inner thoughts and feelings into something visually attractive yet communicative at the same time. If individuals fail to show expressions of desire and expressiveness, they will keep lacking confidence in their abilities.

Thinking unconventionally, however, is the total opposite of conventional thinking. Modern-day designers should express unconventional thinking throughout their performance. By implementing thoughtful ideas, designers will be able to exceed their expectations. Featuring new methods of creative problem solving will help designers accomplish their intentions with quality. Introducing new styles into the design industry will inevitably revive current and future designers. Unconventional thinking could also have an effect on the society if designers are able to achieve implicit results regarding public issues.

A designer's role is to portray a visual message that is effective yet somehow functional at the same time. The purpose of any result is basically to get the attention of a specific target. As creatives, designers are individuals used to executing and collaborating. In order to continue accomplishing successful tasks, creatives should always feel the need to explore. By exploring unfamiliar topics, creatives will gradually be able to generate unconventional thinking. Exploration is the key to creativity; by exploring different aspects, creatives will be able to examine all sorts of compelling subjects; certain subjects that could have a greater effect on the overall performance of a designer and the result which a designer will be after.

To achieve unconventional thinking, designers should demonstrate the eagerness to perform professionally in a creative manner. An unconventional thinker is someone who is willing to take risks and challenge themselves at the same time.

Someone who is confident and always on the lookout for creative trends. An individual who is able to combine creativity with originality. Some ideas may result in failure at times, but that doesn't prevent a creative individual from accomplishing other successful creations. As designers are considered as creatives, inventors, producers, and creators, they are known to have that desire to accomplish prominent results. By implementing unconventional ideas, creatives will be able to express their passion to the public.

A committed designer is someone who is prepared to take on any challenge they face. Any specific challenge or task could release unconventional ideas which designers would be aware of during the design process. It is all up to a designer as an individual to take that slight risk and implement that particular unconventional idea into their actual work. It is essential to keep in mind that unconventional thinking is more like a process. An initial idea unfolds into what is going to be produced by the designer, and so an unconventional production is discovered. With the appropriate thinking and exploration of aspects within the design field, creative individuals will have unceasing opportunities that will continue to flourish always.

Another term creative individuals should pursue is curiosity. Showing an interest and expressing desire to learn something new should always be the priority for creatives. Having the desire to know more and be knowledgeable will act as experience and understanding combined. By being inquisitive, designers will be able to understand more about their profession. Learning from the past will assist designers throughout their design process. An inquisitive designer is someone who perceives valuable information and interprets everything with confidence. Creatives who are well aware of the past will be extremely knowledgeable individuals with an eye for perfection. Inquisitive designers will also impact other creatives from the design field once they begin to demonstrate their skills and abilities towards others.

An individual with inquisitive attributes will be able to maintain innovation. Curiosity will lead individuals to insightful topics and somehow enlighten designers. Creatives with a greater amount of knowledge will have different characteristics compared to common designers. Any knowledge gained throughout a designer's career will end up being beneficial at some stage. Though creatives who are inquisitive will always have an advantage because of their knowledge, once designers evolve into knowledgeable creative individuals, innovation will soon follow. When creatives become fully aware of their profession in terms of understanding and analysing, creatives would then be able to think creatively in an innovatively manner in order to feature new yet original methods.

Innovation in general is all about creative thinking resulting in contemporary creations, where initial ideas are developed with inventiveness. That quality of being inventive will help designers accomplish innovative results all the time. Cultivated designers will always be proficient whenever executing intended plans, and somehow have that extra edge when it comes to professionalism. Innovation is what designers of all levels should pursue. The design industry will only continue to flourish if creative individuals become more eager to create and introduce original ideas of their own. After all, becoming an independent individual when it comes to developing original ideas will aid a designer's strength in achieving imaginative intentions. Relying on others during any design process will affect designers and prevent them from realizing what they are capable of.

Knowledge will surely be vital for any creative willing to kick-start any project, though creatives should always pay attention whenever converting that knowledge into any design. History in general acts as a resource which is available and accessible to designers at all times. Borrowing ideas from actual creations would straight away result in duplication. Designers should be wise enough to know how to use particular sources in order to obtain ideas. Duplication will certainly damage a designer's ability to generate creative thinking. The history of graphic design is an undeniably compelling field filled with interesting facts which could fascinate any designer. Knowing how to use examples of the past wisely will help designers achieve unconventional results.

Also, designers should always attempt to understand and comprehend specific examples before trying to replicate existing productions. Reproducing designs from the past will ruin a designer's ability to think unconventionally, and that is what all creatives should be aware of. There is no point at all in recreating designs that have already been produced at some point in time. Every generation of designers should be able to afford their original and personal thoughts to the industry of design to somehow add their voice and leave a deserving mark of their own. Our industry will only flourish further if unconventional intentions are implemented accurately. Personal characteristics will surely vary from one another, designers as creative individuals would not be able to generate similar thoughts while compared with other creatives.

Passionate designers with a strong will of desire will be able to achieve innovative results without a doubt, though individuals with less self-esteem will never be able to challenge themselves and realise their abilities. Idleness will result in indolent individuals who will eventually distract other creatives and somehow ruin a productive environment. Creative individuals should ignore such distractions and focus solely on their intentions. Seeking innovation requires individuals to be focused at all times, whether it be before or during the design process. Knowledge would certainly provide creative individuals the support they need, by expressing such facts gained into specific designs will result in thoughtful outcomes. The power of knowledge can have a great impact on any creative individual by providing useful information and being enlightened about particular subjects.

Satisfaction is a feeling all designers go through whenever hesitant about a design. Not knowing when to stop or whether what they have created will be pleasing or not are common feelings every designer goes through. Normally, if a designer is unsure about a specific point, they will end up asking for assistance or listening to opinions from other peers. Then the satisfaction feeling settles in, and all of a sudden, the designer becomes satisfied from their production. That moment of satisfaction, however, could terminate creativity from creative individuals. Creatives go through experimental phases during any design process so there is no point panicking at any stage of the process. Panicking during a design process will destroy a designer's potential, from having a bunch of creative unconventional ideas, to becoming uncertain about the actual purpose. Hesitations will eventually continue to overhaul creatives which will affect their confidence straight away.

Creatives, however, should prevent themselves from having second thoughts and instead try to keep going and continue with their intentions. Satisfaction during the design process will lead to incomplete designs, therefore designers should keep on developing their initial ideas until they achieve their objectives one way or another. Creative individuals should express their potential during the development phase of any process. It will be crucial for creatives to keep evolving their original intentions in order to accomplish a complete yet pleasing result. To achieve unconventional results, creatives require special characteristics of eagerness and to always be keen and ambitious. There is a reason why designers are called creatives; that quality of being inventive is a feature all designers should be proud of. Revealing originality in an imaginative way will express creativity in an individual. As creatives, designers should challenge themselves continuously. By overcoming such challenges, designers will be able to control their feelings, knowing that they are on their way to achieve their goals.

Unconventional designers should be individuals with potential, eager enough to develop their abilities with a sense of originality, having the ability to think creatively in order to achieve innovation. Creatives with such characteristics can have an impact on our design industry. By introducing new methods and featuring new styles, the design industry will continue to flourish and attract attention at the same time. Being original reflects on your outcome clearly. Having a voice expressed throughout your productions will result in unique designs that become easily noticed. Perceiving unusual graphics will also reveal unconventional ideas portrayed by the designer. Expressing originality as well will also distinguish a designer amongst others.

To become recognised for something that has been accomplished will be a moment that will be cherished forever.

Designers as individuals should have the mentality to achieve creativity; only with that desire and willingness will designers be able to achieve unconventional results. Creatives are individuals who are knowledgeable and independent. Individuals who know very well what they are capable of achieving. That self-belief will lead creatives to the path of innovation. Coming up with imaginative ideas and implementing those initial ideas will help creatives develop their skills continuously. That development phase will be vital for creatives to understand and experiment during the process of designing. The outcome will surely be rewarding, as creatives will have completed their intentions and plans. Individual attributes differ from one person to another; some designers tend to have that eagerness, yet others lack that specific characteristic. To express unconventional thinking, creatives must enhance their skills further and improve their qualities so that a typical designer evolves to become an unconventional individual who always designs with great passion.

# Chapter 5
## Typography and Linguistic Meaning

Ever imagined a world without letterforms that depict a visual message? Just thinking about visual typographic communication will make anyone realise the importance of such a subject. Typography is one of the major fundamentals of design; a field that involves the arrangements of specific letterforms to express a visual message that combines both creativity and style. A field where art and science collide with one another to form effective yet appealing communication. Perceiving letterforms which are arranged in a particular way somehow translates into a certain language that is being communicated visually. So, basically, language is being transmitted through certain types of arrangements. However, it is vital to keep in mind that any content of typographic means is entirely portrayed as information that serves a purpose, and meaning is being conveyed at the same time.

Designers as creative individuals, on the other hand, relate more to the process of typography, where letterforms become carefully studied. Creating typefaces, selecting certain types, adjusting point sizes and line spacing is what typography is all about from a designer's point of view. It will be certain that any result will convey a message, though it is not up to the designer to have concerns about the meaning being portrayed, since designers are normally commissioned to work out a solution that serves a purpose. Despite being creatives, designers are the individuals who create specific letterforms and arrange them in a way that makes communication legible. Typography will always be the core of any intended design creatives are after. Since visual communication relies on a message that is being portrayed, creatives will always feel the need to include typographic elements. Typography is a field where language collides with creativity to form a visual message. Therefore, arranging letterforms in a creative way will lead to appealing communication designers are after.

As creative individuals, designers go through quite some time to carefully understand a brief and find a suitable solution. The brief, however, being a design problem, is what needs to be solved. A designer's purpose is to find a reasonable answer that visually communicates as a solution, keeping in mind that anything a designer produces must convey a visual message one way or another. That specific visual message is considered to be a vital element for designers. Creative individuals face many design problems of all sorts. From creating a brand identity, designing a packaging line, or even advertising for a certain company, everything a designer produces must contain a visual message that somewhat affects consumers, for creative individuals' typography will always be considered as a primary element whenever designing, having the chance to express their abilities and creativity in arranging particular letterforms in an artistic way to reveal meaningful messages.

Designers also look at typography as a challenging task, since some projects depend solely on typographic elements where a slight mistake could end up being so costly. Revising and closely going through typographic works will reduce common mistakes from occurring and will definitely be to a designer's benefit as well. Especially for designers, it will be unprofessional to produce something that appears to have accidental mistakes, like a misspelled word or a misplaced character which will eventually have an effect on the actual meaning that is being visually conveyed. Preventing particular mistakes from happening will strengthen a designer's understanding of typography in general, and how it is related to communication being transmitted. Also, intensely understanding a field like typography will aid a designer's performance by producing legible creations that have been designed with great thought in mind.

For creatives, it is important to understand that typography has evolved significantly throughout the years. Remarkable creations of typefaces and styles have swept by and influenced our industry vastly, which have led to a developed industry with valuable resources. Some creations are still active today, like Johnston, a typeface designed by Edward Johnston which was commissioned in 1913 for the Underground Electric Railways Company of London. People still walk by that prominent sign every day; Johnston is also still used on maps to guide people through railway lines. It has become part of people's everyday lives just like an essential attachment. The typeface surely doesn't feel dated and truly expresses English style in every factor. Johnston is a typeface known for its clarity because it pleases the eyes from the first moment anyone spots it. This just shows how a specific typeface can influence an entire brand identity all because of appealing typographic figures. Surely certain typefaces can have an effect on a society or even a global effect; it all comes down to how well a creative individual has prepared themselves to face a challenge of such significance.

Ever since Johannes Gutenberg invented the printing press

during the fifteenth century, movable type mechanical printing became widely acknowledged not just across Europe but globally as well. From that moment in time, typography evolved vastly because of the awareness that spread amongst societies. People accepted and appreciated the fact that printed books and materials were accessible to satisfy their needs. From black letter typefaces to old style serifs which then evolved into sans serif typefaces, typographers began inventing creative styles that were mainly intended to communicate yet look attractive at the same time. The invention of a printing press had surely a great effect on the evolution of typography. Not only were typefaces developed with style, but the perception of visual communication became effectively recognizable amongst people.

Also, imagining that printed material was accessible during that period of time will make anyone realise the importance of visual communication and its impact on understanding and perception as a whole. Today, creative individuals use typography as an element more or like as an essential part throughout an expected design process. For creatives, the elements of typography will be crucial during any design process. Trying to create appealing yet expressive results will help creatives achieve their initial intentions. Creatives should also keep in mind that understanding the basics of typography will always be useful towards the implementation process. While implementing ideas, creatives will face challenging tasks regarding portraying an effective message that is meaningful at the same time. Clients will employ or commission designers for the purpose of spreading meaning through certain techniques. For that reason, mainly creative individuals will be responsible to make sure that particular letterforms should interpret the meaning of a certain language that readers can perceive easily.

Speaking of meaning in the typography world will lead to other subtopics creatives should be aware of. Meaning is basically anything that is meant by certain letterforms or words or even ideas and concepts. For creatives who encounter typography as a field all about letterforms, part of their job requires a greater understanding of any context. Producing visually communicative messages that convey meaningful communication will result in a language that is being transmitted. Basically, the study of meaning associated with certain languages is called semantics, a field related entirely to linguistic meaning. Semantics, generally, is considered as the branch that is concerned with linguistics and meaning. In other words, the meaning of texts and arranged letterforms is what semantics is all about.

However, the arrangement of certain words that makes up grammatical sentences in language is called syntax. For creative individuals, acknowledging certain topics might feel pointless or needless at times, because some individuals might think that their role as designers is concerned with implementing creative ideas, though some creative individuals might as well look at it the opposite way. Some topics, however, certainly could not be ignored or disregarded. Especially with semantics, a field with such significance towards the design industry, creatives should demonstrate their inquisitive characteristics in order to succeed as individuals. Therefore, understanding a field like semantics carefully will eventually benefit designers as individuals to become aware of such a subject, yet at the same time aid designers during the design process. Designers as individuals would not want to produce work that lacks meaning; after all, a designer's role is to create visually presented communication that has to be regarded as a solution for a specific problem.

Also, becoming aware of semantics regularly will support designers during the implementation process. Creatives will eventually have an advantage whenever developing visually effective solutions that aim to entice perception while having an impact on behaviour. Whatever designers intend on developing will have to be meaningful in every aspect in order to entice perception in any possible way. Designers will only be able to attain such effective solutions if a complete understanding of such a vital matter is maintained. During any design process, creatives will have to find solutions for certain design problems, and during that process designers must be aware that even though their roles as creatives is to produce appealing yet effective solutions, it has to make sense one way or another to any intended target. A meaningful message is being portrayed visually, which is then perceived by particular audiences. That link of expressive understanding will collide with logic and information, merging with one another to form a language.

Realizing the importance of language through meaning will make anyone comprehend a field like semantics. Designers could not imagine thinking of producing work that lacks meaning, therefore understanding the syntax of English, for example, will prevent grammatical mistakes from occurring whenever designing. For creatives, there will always be subjects yet to be explored, fields of interesting understanding that could transform individuals into curious creatives. Letterforms of basic context are imprecise on their own, somewhat lacking expressiveness whenever presented solely, waiting to be revealed in a way that gets to readers by spreading meaning. Designers are the individuals who create and produce specific solutions that links information to a perceiver. Therefore, digging deep and becoming aware of certain sensitive topics will help creatives produce effective results all the time.

As one of the fundamentals of design, typography is considered as the core of any project. Some designers become so addicted to typography that they realise everything they create, produce, and even wear is type-related. It just shows how much designers as creatives appreciate such a dominant field. That is probably one of the reasons why creatives distinguish typography from other fields, more or like a compelling subject that continues to evoke interest. All successful typefaces begin with initial ideas which are then evolved and developed to specific letterforms. The process of designing typefaces is called type design. Designers of such typefaces go through a long process of development and reviewing of actual drafts.

Making sure that letterforms are legible and suitable will defy particular uses of typefaces. The anatomy of a typeface mainly indicates detailed classification of graphic elements that establish certain fonts from a typeface. Letterforms are also carefully classified and measured upon creating typefaces. Specific names are given for each part of initial letters; this detailed classification of the body which makes up a letterform makes the development process easier for designers. Typography as a field is considered to be a subject all by itself. An art on its own, typography will always act as a major fundamental for designers. Typography is more than the process of arranging type; instead, it is the art of expressing language and understanding through appealing yet artistic results.

Over the years, typography has evolved vastly; styles and movements have affected productions, and therefore designers today have a strong foundation and a base they can rely on, always acting like a reference or a source of information. Type designers today have everything they need to create and design new versions of typefaces. Excuses and obstacles are no longer the issue and have literally become a matter of the past. Information nowadays is accessible to everyone looking to strengthen their understanding of certain topics, especially with a subject like typography. Designers of the modern world have access to many different resources which inevitably help with the design process. Certain tools and software, for example, are available for designers to keep on producing specific designs or typefaces.

Comparing the design process from the fifteenth century with the availabilities of modern-day design will make all creatives appreciate the idea of transformation. Creatives should surely be so grateful that an industry like the design industry has evolved and developed gradually over the years. Time and experience will always reveal greater thinking, which will develop into successful achievements that can eventually transform an industry as a whole on its own. Admiring the distinguished from the past because of their successful achievements has only one explanation, and that is accomplishment. Having achieved something successful will surely have an effect on a creative individual's reputation. A field so dominant as typography has without a doubt evolved throughout the transformation of the creative industry. Styles of specific typefaces have developed throughout the years reflecting on distinct time periods. From Blackletter type to Old Style Serifs, to Slab Serifs and Sans Serifs type, each style has a character of its own. Clearly just going through type specimens of existing typefaces will reveal obvious development of styles used during specific periods of time. What is really appealing with typefaces is the fact that each group of fonts is related to one particular type family (typeface) that has either had an impact on our world or is still active and in use today. This matter just helps us realise truly how typography does not just spread meaningful messages through certain letterforms; instead, typography should be perceived as an effective subject related to science and expressed through design.

Designers as individuals should be well aware of the importance of a field like typography. For creatives, understanding and appreciating the availability of accessible communication gives them greater possibilities of achieving successful results. Achievements of the past will always be considered a foundation or a base for any initial idea. Also, creatives nowadays have the opportunities to explore such accessible information that are regarded as references. Behind every successful yet effective typeface is an eminent individual or type designer. Today, creative individuals should look up to those characters of the past as idols, and aspire to become individuals who are ambitious always and have the desire to achieve success.

Respecting existing typefaces is another matter creatives should pay attention to, always keeping in mind reserved rights whenever placing and adjusting certain typefaces during any design process, for instance, being aware that certain typefaces belong to previous creators or even licensed to some type foundries. Therefore, rights matter, though when it comes to creating designs of your own it is a totally different matter. However, creating designs in a way that is being reproduced and claiming ownership becomes an act of plagiarism clearly; an issue that is truly unacceptable yet unavoidable in our design industry. For designers to clearly understand the importance of rights, individuals must be aware of the importance of visual communication and its impact on our society, becoming aware and conscious of how consumers perceive visual messages that direct and guide their actions. Just grasping that extra thought will help creatives realise how effective a profession like graphic design actually is. Realizing the influence on our society will make designers pay attention even more to whatever they produce. Typography will always be regarded as the base of any effective overall creative outcome, like the key behind a successful project depends on how well a type is constructed and presented. A subject on its own where language collides with creativity just makes it even more interesting. For us creatives, typography will always be the bridge between meaning and imagination where communication becomes processed. Having that opportunity will always give creatives that need and desire to keep on producing visually appealing results that have been carefully thought of.

# Chapter 6
## Readability vs. Legibility

Thinking of employment and vacancies makes you appreciate your role as a designer: a profession so flexible yet so effective. Designers as individuals could be described as lively yet always engaged. Having to accomplish and develop initial ideas requires constant focus and attention. For designers especially, always becoming aware of certain topics helps whenever designing and producing creative ideas. One of the major subjects surrounding the design industry is legibility, which probably most designers get confused about whenever comparing it with readability, another major subject. Designers as individuals should always be aware of such topics related to their profession. Understanding compelling subjects will only act in a designer's favour as an advantage for themselves.

Legibility and readability will always haunt designers whenever producing creative work. Making sure that the message being conveyed is clear and readable will depend on how well designers arrange type. Therefore, typography will always be perceived as an influential matter, and how well it is being produced or arranged all depends on creative individuals. Designers should understand that readability is the quality of easily comprehending letterforms and being able to read with ease. On the other hand, legibility is to do with the clarity of letterforms and the quality of being clear enough for readers. Concerns of mastering readability and legibility techniques rely on the arrangement of particular typefaces. Creatives must widen their knowledge of typefaces and become well aware of a vast amount of typefaces and type families. By becoming knowledgeable, designers will be able to broaden their understanding of type and become aware of certain typefaces that best suit intended projects. For designers, understanding the difference between readability and legibility will always be vital for their own understanding of effective typography. Always keeping in mind that readability is to do with reading, whereas legibility is about recognizing certain typefaces from others will benefit designers during any design process.

Setting type can be difficult at some stages during the design process, especially when designers become confused and hesitant whenever selecting typefaces for specific purposes. Setting type matters greatly towards creative individuals since overall outcomes consisting of type forms should have a direct impact on people in many actual ways. Therefore, creatives will always be responsible for finalised outcomes that aim to entice perception. Responsibility and respect are two terms designers should consider whenever designing with typefaces. Typefaces that are active and accessible in our design industry are all possessed by other creatives. There will always be a right way whenever putting particular type in use, bearing in mind that each existing typeface or font has rights. Therefore, designers will be the ones responsible for anything against their creations. Understanding that typefaces are designed for communication purposes will make creatives aware that respecting any actual typeface will result in appreciation of a typeface's quality.

By respecting a specific typeface, designers will be able to familiarise themselves with the history behind a typeface and its initial purpose. Having a background on certain type designers and their creations will without a doubt broaden a designer's understanding of their field. Also, by becoming familiar with certain typefaces, designers will be able to set type with ease during a design process. The importance of setting type is surely an indispensable subject. Since setting particular letterforms entirely depends on effective results all the time, successful communication totally relies on efficiency whenever setting letterforms. Imagine not reviewing an intended creation and handing it over to a client, then surprisingly realizing that there is an accidental error concerning letter kerning that affects the overall appearance of a specific design. Will that be a designer's responsibility or just an unintentional fault?

When it comes to professionalism, there is no such thing as something unintentional, especially in the design industry. Mistakes happen for different reasons, surely, though designers are creatives who should make sure their creations are always effective and to a high standard. Kerning and leading errors will be noticeable without a doubt; therefore, creatives should always be eager to assess their creations no matter how confident they are. Alignment is another term designers should be aware of whenever setting type. Positioning certain text and arranging letterforms will give designers a different perspective on their intentions. Having specific text aligned and justified will help readers glide visually through any context without complications, and identify words with ease. After all, a designer's role is to produce effective visual communication that always has an impact on particular individuals or a society as a whole or even globally. Despite having other ways of communication and connectivity, visual communication will always be within every aspect. The fact that visual communication is spreading not only through print but digitally as well will give creatives a broader perception of legibility and its effects on readers or perceivers alike. Once creatives have grasped ways of effective communication and the way it is being transmitted, creatives will then be able to implement tested techniques in order to achieve successful communication that is expressible yet intimate at the same time.

Creative individuals should understand the differences between readability and legibility in order to create effective results all the time, being aware that both terms are related to communication that is being conveyed, though both readability and legibility are different from one another when it comes to meaning. Legible words are words you can spot from a distance easily, however this does not mean that legibility is comprehended easily. Mostly logos and signs are legible in every aspect, though picturing the same title or font on a paragraph, for instance, will make readers read in a strenuous way. Readers will require great effort to glide their eyes across sentences, understanding that legible fonts are used for different purposes, and fonts that please the eyes are meant for communication that is continual will clear the differences between both legibility and readability. This is exactly why designers must have the knowledge and experience of typefaces and their history.

Having a strong background about typefaces, their creators, and all the different forms they come in will help creatives through any design process. Also, creatives will gradually build their knowledge regarding an essential subject like typography. Being aware that legibility and readability fall under the field of typography will acquaint creatives even more with such a field. As individuals, designers should understand the basics of type anatomy in order to fully develop techniques that help whenever selecting fonts for different purposes. For example, serif typefaces are known to be more readable in print because of the serifs attached to letterforms, which help readers connect from one letter to another without disturbing the flow of a reader's eye.

On the other hand, sans-serif typefaces are known to be more legible and easily perceived, though not entirely recommended for print purposes, even though sans-serif typefaces appear to be clear and uniformed. This is all based on scientific research and psychology, though it is not necessarily accurate at times. Designers get to make specific decisions that could affect the outcome, and also as individuals are in control of type selections most of the time. Whatever design that is being produced is solely the responsibility of a designer, a creative who becomes accountable for any oversight regarding initial intentions. As creatives, designers should also pay attention whenever aligning type, since common errors may occur without being noticed. Positioning is another term designers should focus on always, since the alignment of letterforms greatly influences visual perception. Communicative forms would not be successfully conveyed if typographic forms are not positioned effectively. Whether designing with serif or sans-serif typefaces, designers should be aware that whatever is being produced has to convey a message of sorts. Finding a solution from the beginning and relying on research will certainly be useful later on during the design process.

Creatives could argue continuously whenever trying to decide on a typeface, like an ongoing debate that has to be settled. It will always be frenetic, because designers are creatives, and certain topics regarding typography matter greatly because decisions yet to be made are decisive most of the time. Typefaces are available and accessible for designers to enhance their developments in order to have an impact on people. Therefore, it will always be difficult for designers to settle and decide on a specific typeface for their projects, though trying to explore different typefaces each time will surely give designers a broader understanding of what type suits each project best. This process will help creatives whenever selecting typefaces for intended projects, because designers have already experienced and tested certain typefaces so that presumptions become much clearer. Creatives will also be able to have expectations of how their intentions will turn out after the design process.

Exploring different styles will only benefit an individual and raise experience levels so that designers become more proficient at their profession. There are loads of typefaces to choose from, and each typeface is so special for many different reasons. Whether selecting the likes of Adrian Frutiger's 'Univers', Max Miedinger and Eduard Hoffmann's 'Helvetica', and Eric Gill's 'Gill Sans' for a sans-serif based design, or going for a more classical feel, with serif typefaces like William Caslon's 'Caslon', John Baskerville's 'Baskerville', Claude Garamond's 'Garamond', and Giambattista Bodoni's 'Bodoni', each and every typeface is so unique in its own way. These are just examples of some of the most notable and recognised typefaces, though there are many other typefaces of the same standards and fame. Type designers who have achieved successful yet effective results in the past have been and always will be recognised for their accomplishments. Not only because of their creations, but because of the impact they have spread amongst generations of people. These certain typefaces have influenced generations of people and creatives alike and will continue to influence future generations to come. Effective accomplishments will also continue to inspire creatives to create visual communication that has been influenced by the past. Having an instant influence on a society will soon unfold into a global effect, and once an individual has reached that level of appreciation, respect and admiration will be inevitable without a doubt.

Whenever designing with type, designers should be aware of complexity in order to produce effective solutions. Certain typefaces are meant for specific purposes, so, for designers, understanding the basics will surely be beneficial later on during the design process. Making sure that results are legible and totally comprehensible will ease complications a designer might face. Creatives should also keep in mind that communication is being transmitted through intelligible and legible words. Readability is the ability to read in order to understand the message being conveyed, whereas legibility is to do with perceiving type and becoming aware of it, though it does not necessarily communicate. People of our modern world require guides that direct their everyday lives. Living in a world without visual communication that directs and guides people to accomplish their needs would be meaningless and ineffective. Therefore, the role of designers is to spread communication that is visually perceived and expressed to consumers in need of awareness and guidance.

Communicative solutions are so effective and compelling yet irresistible at times whenever results are so seductive. No one can ever imagine a world without words or communication, a place with no direction or appealing influences. One reason why creatives should appreciate their profession is because of how influential and effective a profession like graphic design actually is. Designing an advertisement campaign, for instance, requires alluring and convincing solutions for a result to be successful. The same goes on whenever designing a packaging line for a food label; finished products have to be alluring so that consumers become attracted to the object. This impact on people is called effective communication, which could either be legible or readable depending on certain projects and outcomes. This sort of influence on people is so satisfying for designers, because it feels like a victorious accomplishment where creatives become credited for their productions.

Achieving effective communication requires concentration and understanding. Knowing how to set type, what type communicates best, and how communication should be transmitted will surely be the key to achieve visual communication that has an effect on people. After all, a design's success depends solely on the designer; the outcome will either end up being successful or not. Certain aspects will clearly determine how effective a particular design can or cannot be. One major aspect will be the representation of type, and the possibility of influencing a society or any intended target. Therefore, designers should always follow rules and guidelines whenever designing, and above all to have respect towards the creators of the past whenever using existing elements. Designing with respect and responsibility will give creatives the confidence to produce effective work.

Overall, being aware of readability and legibility whenever designing will open up different solutions for creatives. Presenting letterforms in a way that spreads communication will be a great responsibility only creatives with knowledge should encounter. A subject so important that it could literally affect consumers and users alike. Only creatives will have the authority and will be the ones who make final decisions towards type representations. Also, creatives will have full and complete control of setting type so that it is being represented and presented in an appropriate way. Realizing that letterforms should be set to please the eyes yet convey a message at the same time will help creatives grasp the importance of effective typography. Implementing layouts that are both readable and legible will also help creatives explore different styles during a design process. Experiencing certain styles is one way to strengthen a designer's ability to produce innovative ideas.

Since readability and legibility fall under a major design fundamental like typography, unconventional thinking will always be vital for creatives during and after a design process. Trying to think in an unconventional way will aid a designer's ability to produce fresh and imaginative ideas in the field. Creatives will eventually be able to process innovative ideas and begin implementing their visions. Also understanding that legible typography does not always support readability since distinct type forms may at times be difficult to read whenever applied for textual content though successfully perceived from a distance. Trying out different styles and exploring through letterforms is one inevitable way that benefits creatives and strengthens their abilities. Researching and exploring topics and people related to a certain field will broaden an individual's thinking and play a major role when it comes to decision making. An imaginative designer will have specific characteristics to develop individual skills and techniques to evolve into an experienced professional who is able to perform efficiently without complications.

Someone who is professional is someone who is able to produce work at the highest level with continuous efficiency.

An individual who is responsible for the outcome of designs. Responsibility is a vital state creative should always consider. Being aware that creative solutions could affect people and also spread awareness around societies shows how visual communication can be effective. The impact that could spread globally all depends on the design problem and the creative individual, therefore making sure that the message being transmitted should be effective will be the key to successful influence. Also understanding that readability and legibility can play a major role whenever working with communication will help creatives realise how effective visual communication can be.

Readability and legibility are two terms designers should always keep in mind whenever designing. Both are different from one another, though both terms are related to the same field. Typography is the field of letterforms, and how particular letters are being displayed matters greatly. Whether type is presented artistically or uniformly, a language is always being transmitted. For a language to have an effect, letterforms should appear in a readable and legible form which should always look appealing. The arrangement of type is more than an art, it is a language that is conveyed and most importantly a way of life. Displaying letterforms so that they communicate should be regarded as an influential matter. So effective that no one can live without. If only people would appreciate the fact that their lives depend on communication and directions; graphic design would always be perceived as an effective profession. Clearly no one could imagine living a life without letters and a language to communicate with, surely.

# Chapter 7
## The Three Cs of Graphic Design

Graphic design is regarded as the creative industry where innovation collides with originality to produce imaginative solutions that influence others. Designers will always be perceived as creative thinkers, though not all designers produce the same level of work. Each and every creative individual has their own way of solving design problems. But, most importantly, each creative has a different experience towards such a compelling field like graphic design. Any particular approach from a designer will express a certain amount of knowledge and understanding they have maintained previously or are currently aware of. Becoming aware of specific terms related to the design field will bolster an individual's character and help to strengthen their abilities, just like a support tool which helps to reinforce a certain solution and makes it feel complete.

Before beginning a design process, creatives should consider terms like composition, components, and concept, or, in other words, the three Cs of graphic design. In order to prevent obstacles during a design process, creatives must be aware of layouts, elements, and ideas that act as part of a complete design. Understanding that composition is to do with the layout of an intended design, components are what make up a complete design, and a concept is an overall idea behind a finished design that will help creatives realise the importance of structure. Since all successful designs depend on well-structured layouts which include particular elements that gradually build up an initial idea, and eventually form a completed effective solution. The relationship behind the three Cs of design is pretty clear and straight forward, though mostly ignored by most creatives of the modern day. Taking the time to generate ideas and gradually form a concept that includes certain elements and components will eventually result in an arranged yet organised layout which helps ease the design process on a designer who faces a task to complete. Designers as creative thinkers are meant to produce effective designs and solutions that influence people one way or another. Therefore, paying attention to composition, components, and concept will aid designers and strengthen their abilities during any design process creatives might face.

Setting and form are considered to be vital aspects of a complete design. Acknowledging that composition defines a finished design will be crucial for designers whenever designing. Literally, composition is to do with the layout of an intended design and how it is made up to completion. Setting certain components in a specific way builds up a design gradually. Of course, developing a design into different phases is a common process amongst designers, though the setting and layout is actually what is being developed to satisfy clients or designers alike. How a design might look or how it is presented is all based on a specific layout a designer has set right from the beginning of any design process. Form, however, is related to the appearance of particular elements in a design which is finished and completed. The way that certain components exist or are presented is what form is all about. Basically, setting is more like a process every designer goes through one way or another.

On the other hand, form is like an evaluation that only occurs upon a design's completion. What matters most about composition is appearance and presentation, because the way a designer presents their final creation will be decisive when it comes to success. It is all up to designers to present and arrange elements in a way that is appropriate yet still effective. Grid systems are also common amongst designers, a process where grids are developed to identify a specific layout before beginning the design process. For many designers, grids are known to be an experimental phase where creatives try different styles and arrangements that typically identify what the final design would look like. Creatives use grids to help with alignment and visual hierarchy. Developing and testing different alignments is all part of the design process. After all, designers will be the ones responsible for any outcome.

Whatever is presented and perceived has to be considered and well thought about. Composition by all means can play a major part in a design's style. Movements and styles of the past have based their creations on particular grids and layouts that have become known since being produced and introduced. De Stijl and the Bauhaus movements, for instance, are significant examples of styles that have had huge influences on composition. Well-structured grids and layouts can have an impact on style in order to identify a particular technique or method for creatives to try and attempt. Certain grids and layouts today have been introduced decades ago, yet designers of today still find specific layouts so intriguing. Composition is without a doubt considered to be a major aspect of design. Designers as creative individuals should try to attempt unconventional ways to create well aligned and uniformed designs which are effective at the same time. Composing a design so that it appears appealing requires skill and technique, designers however are creatives who are able to encounter such a challenging task. Therefore, it will always be vital for creatives to keep in mind that one part of success depends solely on composition itself.

Another major aspect of design is the components a particular design includes such as type, colour, and shape. Basically, whatever makes up an initial design is regarded as components which eventually complete the appearance. Some designs might consist of just one component, whereas other designs might include three or four components. Decisions are totally controlled by designers after all. Components in a design actually build up a complete design, though creatives become in control of quantity and size. Some creatives regard the selection of components to be more like a decision-making phase, whereas other creatives regard it as an experimental phase. It all comes down to how well creatives have prepared themselves to construct and develop their initial ideas, since decision-making and experimenting is all part of the design process which every designer should go through one way or another.

Thinking of components a design should include sounds easy, though most designers tend to struggle and somehow miss out on accessible elements that have been forgotten about and disregarded. Dismissing certain elements and focusing on a handful will prevent innovation. Creatives should always consider a change and accept new challenges they are not used to, especially when it comes to deciding what elements to include in a design. For designers, accessible elements are never ending because as creatives, designers are also able to design their own elements like patterns, fonts, and shapes. Available options are truly vast, and for that reason everyone expects high standards from designers. Any component a design includes should be innovative and imaginative in one way or another. Designers as creative individuals have inventive characteristics that should be challenged either way. Challenging oneself will strengthen an individual mentally and reveal proficient attributes which express professionalism.

Creative skills will only develop if an individual accepts to overtake a challenge, just like a creative idea that evolves gradually to produce a solution which is controlled by the designer. Creative skills and techniques can develop even further if only designers become more willing to test their abilities. Experimenting with different elements is one simple way to challenge creative skills gained by designers. Testing one's abilities is also another way to develop individual skills and characteristics. As creative individuals, designers are capable of continuously developing individual characteristics based on certain challenges they have encountered. Since each individual faces varying challenges, experience levels will also vary amongst designers. Therefore, for creatives it will always be vital to experiment with different elements a design might consist of, since experimenting is also part of any design process that gradually develops initial ideas into effective results.

Creatives must go through a variety of accessible elements to find out what best suits them in order to solve a problem. After all, any component a design consists of has already been approved by none other than designers themselves, who have eventually developed what a complete design would end up looking like. So, for consumers or users to approve the effectivity from a particular design, creatives must make sure that any result must communicate in a visual manner. Any component a specific design includes must spread a visual message that reaches out to an audience. Creatives are surely the ones responsible for the effectiveness of a design, though part of any impact towards consumers relies on whatever a design consists of, which one way or another helps to spread communication. Certain aspects of a design express the character of the designer who will always be the individual in charge of any outcome. For creatives, the importance of visual appearance should be greatly considered and studied whenever designing.

Evolving a particular design requires creative intelligence from a creative individual. For a design to gradually develop during any design process, creatives must generate ideas in order to form a concept which is the base of any complete design. A concept can be described as an idea which initially unfolds to become a plan, that somehow turns out to be a designer's intention. An initial thought which normally occurs upon receiving a design brief is regarded as part of a concept. Trying to picture how a finished design might look or what elements to include in order to produce a solution is all part of building a concept. For creatives, a concept is regarded as the balance of a complete design. Concepts gradually develop during the beginning of a design process before designers even begin designing. The amount of knowledge and information will benefit designers greatly whenever developing a concept. Therefore, researching well and preparing for a task will be crucial for creative individuals whenever generating ideas. Creatives should also attempt to set an aim which one way or another helps creatives maintain focus throughout the development phase. Only a complete design will speak for its concept, therefore creatives must prioritise their intentions in order to achieve their goals.

Each creative individual is gifted in their own way, so the process of generating ideas differs from one individual to another. Experience levels also matter greatly because of the amount of understanding and information an individual retains. For instance, a first-year design student can't be compared with a fourth-year design student, since first-year students just begin to develop individual skills and gain knowledge whereas final-year students have already been acquainted with useful information and are well aware of their profession. The same goes on with designers in practice, where experience levels differ totally from one designer to another. Individual abilities should not be compared at all times, since knowledge and information only will state one's capabilities by revealing an individual's potential. Creatives should always demonstrate eagerness and willingness whenever expressing creativity in order to inspire generations of designers to come. Acting as aspiring individuals will lead to ambitious generations that thrive one way or another.

Generating ideas is considered to be a tough task at some stage of a designer's career, though it is all up to the designer to react instantly and ignore any distractions that might prevent creativity. Developing ideas even further will help creatives achieve their intentions without preventing originality. Creatives should realise that a concept is more than just an initial idea. A concept amongst creatives should be regarded as an imaginative intention from a creative individual that gradually develops to become a solution. Forming a concept requires innovative thinking and constant researching in order to be capable of generating creative thoughts. Having a concept while designing will direct and lead creatives during the design process so that intentions are achieved. Creatives should always be well informed and prepared to face any task they might encounter at any point. Facing unexpected moments requires sophisticated individuals who are dependable at all times.

Designers as creative individuals base their creations on imaginative thoughts that gradually evolve into intentions. Initial ideas are specified as the foundation of any complete design. Creatives should understand that in order to achieve successful results, producing creative ideas is the key to gradually developing specific designs. Without thoughts and ideas, creatives would not be able to form innovative solutions. During the design process, creatives would require certain skills that can benefit individual performances. Becoming aware of the three Cs of graphic design will help creatives perform smoothly without any complications. Understanding terms like composition, components, and concept will broaden an individual's thinking and expand their understanding even more.

Designers should be aware that successful designs depend on well-structured layouts. Also, that form and appearance matter as much as elements and ideas do. The appearance of a particular design and the distribution of specific elements should be considered to be vital aspects of a complete design too. Also, designers as creatives should experiment to the utmost levels in order to achieve inventive solutions. Experimenting with composition, for example, will lead to countless layouts and options to choose from. Symmetrical layouts, for instance, are made up of identical parts of both sides facing each other. Showing symmetry will result in well-uniformed and structured layouts. On the other hand, asymmetrical layouts are totally the opposite of symmetrical layouts where objects or components are arranged in an irregular manner, where parts fail to correspond with one another and appear to lack symmetry in size, shape, or arrangement. Testing out symmetrical and asymmetrical layouts will strengthen individual skills and help creatives experience original solutions.

Defining the perimeter whenever designing is another way to experiment with composition. To define the perimeter of a specific design, creatives test out different layouts to fill any blank space available, which is regarded as the perimeter or the area of margin space. There are two ways to fill a perimeter so that elements appear clearly. A passive perimeter allows viewers to focus on the elements within a specific layout. Usually, elements in a passive perimeter are centred or distributed within the empty space in a layout, though an active perimeter pulls away the attention of perceivers and allows elements to flow over the margins in a continuous way. Layouts that are based on an active perimeter normally lead the eyes off a page, feeling like a sequence. Creatives are known to be reliable individuals who are able to produce innovative solutions. Therefore, experimenting with the fundamentals of design will only be in regard of a creative's benefit. At the same time, creatives would have developed individual skills and established personal attributes along the way. This is why knowledge and information are considered to be significant towards designers.

Developing individual skills will improve designers as creative individuals. Seeking knowledge will also result in wise individuals who are able to perform at the highest levels. Gradually developing individual skills will also lead to professionalism which only passionate designers are after. Expressing passion towards one's profession will lead to desire and the feeling of wanting to achieve something. Only individuals with pure passion will thrive to become successful. As creative individuals, designers should always express will and desire whenever designing or researching. Wishing to accomplish initial ideas will help designers achieve more than a client's approval.

Experience would be the right word to describe anything achieved by a designer. Developing experience requires constant practice in order to distinguish skill from knowledge. Understanding the three Cs of graphic design will help creatives develop designs with ease, and most importantly to picture the outcome while implementing such understanding. Paying attention to composition, components, and concept during the design process will surely guide creatives through the development process. By gradually forming a concept and becoming aware of the visual appearance, designers will be able to picture and visualise the outcome of an intended design. Feeling what a design might or will look like is all part of the design process. Therefore, as creatives, designers should always be well prepared to face any task that might come their way. The process of composing a design requires well informed individuals who are practical in a way about solving a problem while finding a suitable solution.

Creatives should try and enlighten themselves in order to expand their understanding of their profession. Considering vital terms like composition, components, and concept will be favourable in many ways for designers. Not only would such terms widen an individual's knowledge, but also add value and appreciation to the purpose of designing and creating visually communicative results. Therefore, as creative individuals, designers should express their passion towards their profession in order to achieve innovation and become successful individuals. After all, designers are individuals with vast yet unique abilities; individuals who are gifted with creativity yet are also able to synthesize. Capabilities differ from one person to another, though demonstrating will and desire will greatly benefit individual characteristics in order to be productive. With such characteristics, creatives will be able to achieve beyond their expectations.

# Chapter 8
## Embracing Creativity

Designers as individuals are seen as creative individuals with great abilities. The term creative refers to the innovative capability a designer acquires during practice. A profession where initial ideas are developed into visually communicative productions helps creative individuals obtain such skills. In order to succeed at a profession of such, designers must always be eager enough to develop individual skills in order to have effective results all the time. The process of generating ideas that are imaginative yet original requires curiosity and awareness of particular subjects. Since designers can't function without creativity, the process of developing ideas might be difficult at times when designers are not prepared for a task. Therefore, for creatives to become successful at solving a design problem, creatives must embrace creativity. To think creatively or to produce creative results, designers must find an inspiration, which will one way or another have an instant effect on one's thinking and aid the process of generating ideas.

To keep up generating ideas constantly is a tough task, therefore designers should always develop their understanding in order to manage the flow of imaginative and original ideas of all sorts. The importance of creativity will only be realised when a project or task is completed, when the actual designer becomes the judge who evaluates an outcome. By realizing the amount of work and research put into a particular project, designers gradually realise that without an initial idea there would not be a result. Going through the development phase and producing effective results will help designers consider their decisions for future projects. Creative thoughts and ideas are considered to be the starting point of any design process. For creatives to develop creative thinking skills, constant practice will be required to maintain high standards. Reconsidering the fundamentals of design and having a broad understanding will help strengthen a designer's overall performance. Creative individuals should embrace creativity by all means in order to keep on producing and generating creative ideas that matter. By expressing willingness, creatives will be able to obtain and control creative measures whenever needed.

At times, creative thinking could be risky, not because certain ideas are imaginative but because most original ideas have not been tested or experimented with yet. Normally, tested ideas are guaranteed for designers, and are somewhat considered as safe to try. However, by being inventive, designers become in control of handling unexpected situations and circumstances, which will result in absolute decision making that will one way or another strengthen leadership skills in an individual. Having total control will also help improve a designer's understanding by becoming more aware of unconventional topics. Comparing creative thinking with strategic thinking will help creatives realise the importance of developing initial ideas, which will eventually result as the solution creatives are after.

To have a strategy, creatives must have an aim or goal to achieve. A plan that is applied by a creative individual in order to achieve certain goals and targets is what strategic thinking is all about. So, the process of achieving an aim differs greatly from the process of inventing innovative yet original ideas, though both processes are regarded as vital aspects of the design field. In order for creatives to balance between creativity and strategizing, individuals must try to challenge their abilities to produce satisfying and rewarding results. Accepting unpredicted challenges will benefit creative individuals greatly by reinforcing knowledge. Balancing creativity with strategic thinking throughout a design process will straight forwardly result in efficient quality being produced by designers. Efficiency will always be required from creatives in the design industry, whether performing at the highest level or not. A creative profession such as design demands individuals to always be organised and competent; individuals who maximise their efforts in order to be productive. Such characteristics will surely make a difference towards a designer's performance. An efficient designer will be clearly identified amongst others, not just because of evident performances but also because of an obvious style that gradually develops overtime; a style which clearly expresses experience and professionalism through every part of a process.

Becoming a mature creative who is independent and capable of facing design problems of all sorts should be what designers aspire to become. Having a willingness and desire to attain and achieve efficient characteristics will help creatives shape their identities. There will be moments in time, of course, where creatives face obstacles and might even doubt their abilities, but such hurdles in life occur for a reason, and as creatives, such obstacles should be seen as a positive reason to improve individual attributes by learning from such experiences.

Creatives should always try to overcome certain difficulties that might be faced, in order to prevent any effects that might impact the generation of ideas. To keep up with generating ideas creatives must enlighten themselves even more. To constantly develop understanding, creatives must be inquisitive, since the process of generating ideas would not be successful without suitable knowledge obtained by individuals. Combining two vital ways of thinking throughout a design process will aid designers in producing effective results. Understanding that creative thinking is related to strategic thinking when it comes to developing initial ideas whenever designing will help creatives realise the importance of developing certain ideas in order to achieve a goal or an intention.

Being aware that creative thinking will one way or another lead designers to form a plan, which will gradually develop thinking skills in order to transform and become a strategy will be necessary for designers during a design process, since developing ideas further down the line will benefit designers greatly by producing creative results that will somehow influence others. After all, a designer's purpose is to have an effect on people, communities, and societies. So, influencing other individuals would be tough to achieve without certain skills and understanding related to creativity and innovation. Therefore, creative individuals should be prepared whenever facing any challenges that might be encountered. Creatives will always be the ones responsible for any outcome. So, being assured that any specific result has been fully developed using particular ways of thinking will be the key factor to success.

Before an implementation process actually begins, designers must go through the development process. The word 'develop' in our design industry clearly refers to the advancement and progression of creative ideas. Either way, as creatives, designers must experience such a phase before and after an actual design process. Developing creative ideas from an inspiration or an initial idea will help creatives achieve personal goals set from the beginning. Every complete design would have been developed into different stages before appearing as a final presented result. It is up to a designer to control the development process of an actual design, because designers are the only ones dealing with adjustments until a design feels complete to be presented. So, for designers to understand how far developing a project may go for, creatives must incorporate client needs and somehow try to understand what exactly their initial intentions are. By being aware of the purpose, designers will be able to limit themselves during a development process. Being in charge will make creatives feel more liable towards anything they might produce. Responsibility will only strengthen individual characteristics and have an impact on confidence. Undeniably confident designers will have an extra edge and will also look more self-assured whenever dealing with clients.

Constantly being active will also raise inspiration levels and help designers become more influenced by their surroundings and be easily inspired. Creative inspirations will eventually develop into inventive ideas that will greatly affect a designer's performance. Frequency will directly spark creativity; by being active more frequently, designers will be able to think more creatively so that ideas evolve with quality. One of the best ways to keep ideas flowing is by being active more regularly. By being more active, designers get to accomplish greater results that will aid productivity. At times it might be difficult for some designers to be engaged by work which requires client services, however, other options are also available for creatives who are without actual work. For example, setting a creative task each day will help boost activity levels in a designer. A particular task set by a creative individual can be anything, literally. Whether a task calls for photographing a specific subject or accomplishing a hike somewhere, it doesn't have to be design related when it comes to inspiration, since inspiration may strike anywhere at any place. It is that specific feeling where a designer feels inspired to create something that actually matters.

So, being constantly active will influence designers one way or another. It all comes to how designers react to personal feelings which requires determination to be activated. Therefore, maintaining creativity will be vital for designers whenever developing creative ideas, since any final result will depend entirely on creative skills designers have obtained prior to designing, understanding that a development process does not only begin whenever designing, but instead the starting point begins right when an inspiration strikes. This sort of thinking will be crucial for creatives whenever trying to comprehend the actual design problem they are about to face. Creatives should be aware that developing creative ideas that have originally sparked from inspirations even further will benefit the outcome greatly yet also be useful for creatives to actually understand the purpose of designing.

For creatives, a profession like design requires constant thinking skills which gradually evolves into creative productions. The process of evolving ideas that crosses a designer's mind will aid a creative individual's production abilities. By being productive, designers become more active by producing and creating innovative results. The importance of being productive will not only be in regard of individual attributes, though productivity will be the key to generating creative ideas. Constantly producing creative solutions whether it is for clients or even individual preferences will result in active designers who are well engaged. For creatives to actually understand the influences of productivity on creativity, creatives must experience certain tasks which support activity. Also, productivity will one way or another broaden a designer's thinking and somehow strengthen individual characteristics, which will have an effect on performance levels.

Being aware of particular subjects that designers might come across while being active will be useful at some point during a different stage. Designers will either gain knowledge by expanding their understanding or become self-assured individuals who are confident in their abilities. Either way, the purpose of being productive will, without a doubt, benefit individual features yet, most importantly, trigger creative objectives a designer might have. Since creatives are individuals who are able to produce inventive creations that are effective by merging original and imaginative ideas to form visually appealing results which communicates. Thus, productivity would not be considered a tough task from a creative's point of view. Basically, any result a designer produces or tends to produce is known to be the solution to a cause or aim that has been identified prior to designing from the designer.

Initially, creatives create to make an impact and influence others. Therefore, the aim of being productive is to be able to produce results which are effective in a continuous manner. For instance, designing a pattern would be a very straight-forward task that is merely uncomplicated. Though, has anyone ever thought about the vast selections of productions a single pattern can evolve into? A basic pattern of any shape can be transformed into certain apparel, printed on stationery, or even used on furniture. The wide range of varieties available to experiment with will be useful for creatives to experience creative productions. What actually matters is how designers react whenever producing solutions. Each creative individual thinks differently, as a result comparing characteristics would not be appropriate whenever trying to evaluate a designer. Creatives must believe in their capabilities in order to achieve innovative results. By expressing desire, creatives will be able to achieve more than their expectations. It does not matter how each individual reacts to productivity, what really matters is the creative outcome which has been produced by a designer. The time and thought put together in order to accomplish a creative goal will be significant towards the outcome.

Another vital aspect which all eager creatives should consider is enlightenment. The state of being enlightened by greater knowledge and understanding will change the way a designer obtains information. Expanding knowledge requires time and patience surely, though it is totally up to an individual to express the effort needed to broaden that understanding. Becoming aware of certain subjects will not only be useful for information purposes, but creative individuals would also become more independent and unconstrained by their awareness levels. Becoming acquainted with knowledge will also support creatives greatly by aiding the process of unconventional thinking which most aspiring designers should be after. Surely, there are many ways for designers to gain knowledge and information in order to broaden their understanding. Specific places like libraries or museums, for instance, are basic places for creatives to look for interesting topics and subjects that might influence or inspire designers, though other ways of enlightening oneself are also available at reach.

Books, for example, have been ignored by most designers nowadays. Some designers would think that reading about design topics would just be a waste of time, instead of a way that might revitalise thinking. A vast selection of books from various design writers are available at nearly every bookstore. Though that indolent feeling still keeps attacking designers silently, reading about what other designers have to say about graphic design, for instance, will help creatives realise different matters that have not actually crossed their own minds. Design-related books offer topics not only about a profession, but also case studies and inspirational works are also presented. Exploring different perspectives will affect creative individuals instantly. Just coming across unexpected topics will be an advantage at some point in a creative's career. Looking for information in order to gain knowledge will give creatives the confidence and belief whenever accepting a challenge. Therefore, always feeling the need to become an inquisitive individual will have a great impact on creatives. Constant researching about interesting topics will also make creative individuals feel enlightened.

By looking for information, creatives basically implement researching skills without even noticing. Since researching is regarded as a main design fundamental, creatives should always tend to express their interests in exploring advanced topics and subjects they are not aware of. In order to gain greater knowledge, creatives must always be patient, since developing understanding requires time to settle and endure. Creatives should always try to enlighten themselves about subjects not only related to their profession, but also subjects that are related to their surroundings. Becoming an individual who is well aware of their surroundings will also have an influence on other individuals because of being a well-informed character. An enlightened individual becomes known straight away amongst other individuals. That sort of impression which eventually affects others will be vital for the design industry as a whole, since inspiring others with nothing other than knowledge will be the key to producing inventive solutions all the time.

Overall, creativity as a subject is so compelling and interesting to look into. The implementation of imaginative yet original ideas will gradually evolve into a creative production; a simple process which is controlled by no one other than creative individuals, which is why retaining creative skills will depend on desire and willingness from creative individuals. Only creatives can control the generation of certain ideas which eventually affects creativity. Therefore, developing thinking skills constantly will help designers achieve creative results without complications. Also, by being productive, designers will be able to produce vast selections of inventive ideas, which will one way or another influence individual qualities.

Having an effect on one's soul will be crucial towards producing creative results. Therefore, being influenced by surroundings will be essential for creatives to begin thinking creatively. The importance of creativity should be clear and direct right from the beginning of a designer's career. In order for creatives to be aware of such importance, creatives must challenge their abilities in order to witness their capabilities. Only results of creative solutions produced by designers will decide the amount of creativeness a designer obtains. There is always room for improvement in the design industry. By being active continuously, creatives will be able to develop creative skills even further down the line, hence always having the desire and will to produce creative solutions will greatly affect any outcome, of sorts. Gaining inspiration from unexpected places will help creatives realise that creativity occurs for a reason, and such personal thoughts are greatly influential on a designer's perspective. To enhance creativity in our everyday lives as creatives, we must think of what or how we should be influenced by our surroundings. A slight incident or thought will surely have an impact on creatives; it is the thoughtful insights which have been explored by creatives that actually matter. The more creatives analyse a subject, the more effective they will end up being.

# Chapter 9
# Being Imaginative

Individual features differ from one person to another; as creatives, most designers require certain attributes in order to become more successful at their profession. Surely some features naturally develop over time, though, for creatives specifically, certain characteristics require a vast amount of effort and constant activity. Considering what the public thinks or expects from designers normally sounds surprising, since random people normally think of designers as creators only. For most creatives such comments will hurt eventually, however creatives should be prepared and set to face such incidents. By demonstrating and revealing individual attributes constantly, designers become more confident and assertive. Having a confident character will affect a creative's performance because of what others think. Creatives should never be seen as behind-the-scenes individuals. It all comes down to the public and how they perceive creatives. Leaving an impression requires determined effort in order for individual characteristics to be revealed.

A profession like design is much more than creating for others; the impact designers have on societies is great in many ways, though to make sure that such an impact is always regarded by others is actually what matters. Influencing others on a daily basis without even realizing their effects on people would not help designers understand their roles as creatives.

Being aware of the purpose behind an approach like visual design will benefit creatives immensely. Designers will realise that developing visually communicative results that are meaningful in every aspect are quite vital towards people's functions. Most importantly, such results will direct people to follow individual paths in a way that guides them to perform whatever they intend on, all because of being directed visually by communicative results. Such thought will help creatives understand the reason for producing effective solutions. Expressing creativity in many ways helps designers become more imaginative. To become active more regularly will be beneficial towards creatives; creatives will also gain even more creative skills. By developing creative skills gradually, creatives become able to produce unconventional ideas our design industry needs. Introducing new ways of thinking, whether it is related to inspirations or facts, will be useful for designers at some stage of any design process basically. Since designers are creative individuals who express creative skills in order to achieve visually communicative results, individual features will be vital in order to succeed.

Everyone agrees that designers are regarded as creative thinkers; in order to be creative, designers must reveal individual features. Creativity is far from just creating artistic solutions; creatives should understand that creativity is all about the use of imagination and originality to produce effective solutions. By expressing imaginative skills, creatives reveal their talents by generating unconventional ideas. Imagination will have an effect on creative individuals, by leading creatives to gradually develop innovative and unconventional ideas. Becoming inspired by certain surroundings or specific objects that crosses a designer's mind will lead creatives to generate certain ideas as well. Realizing what designers are capable of achieving will help creatives understand how essential a profession like graphic design actually is.

Creatives have the ability to create meaningful results, though creatives should not cease skills obtained from the past. Improving and developing individual characteristics by gaining more experience and knowledge will help creatives gain even more useful skills. Surely, at times, creatives will face difficulties achieving specific goals, the main reason for such a state will be struggling to generate ideas. Eventually, every designer will go through an experience of such, though it is completely up to the designer to find a solution and solve this phase. By inspiring oneself, a creative becomes more refreshed mentally. The ability to think and generate original ideas naturally refreshes and revives by none other than creative individuals themselves. With effort and will, creatives will be able to develop thinking skills in order to achieve innovative results constantly without any distractions. Once creatives maintain such thinking skills, ideas will begin to flow naturally.

It all comes down to how well a creative individual has prepared themselves to begin being imaginative. The purpose of generating imaginative yet innovative ideas is connected to the success of an initial idea. Without an initial idea, creatives would not be able to develop imaginative ideas further. Eventually, particular ideas make up an original design. Therefore, in order to become successful at achieving imaginative solutions, creatives must be aware of the reason for design. Asking questions like: Why is this design important? Who is the intended target? How will a creative solution affect others? will be useful for designers whenever they are trying to find ideas or before beginning a design process. Becoming aware of the main reason behind an intended creative result will benefit creatives greatly by making them understand more about the final effect of a solution. Creatives will eventually understand and realise the reason to produce an effective result. By combining original yet imaginative thoughts and ideas, creatives will be able to achieve innovative results that will have an impact on a certain group of people. The sort of influence creatives will have on others will depend solely on the success of a result. Therefore, creatives should always be prepared whenever receiving a design brief, and by implementing all the essential fundamentals whenever designing, creatives will be able to attain their intentions without complications.

Imagination is a word with two meanings, originally. Fortunately, both meanings are related to designers in some way or another. Most creatives think of imagination as the ability to form creative ideas from the mind, though most creatives do not pay attention to the fact that imagination also reflects the part of the brain which imagines things. Creatives should realise that whenever trying to visualise any design prior to designing, creatives naturally enter an imagining phase. Whenever designers try to visualise the outcome or expected designs, the mind naturally imagines things (in this case it is the outcome of an intended design). By visualizing more often, creatives will gradually develop decision-making skills. Trying to imagine how the final result might look will benefit designers greatly by having an idea of what the outcome will end up like. Also, creatives will be able to determine what kind of composition or style to go for during a design process. By visualizing the outcome as well, creatives will be able to decide on what elements to go for while designing. Visualizing the outcome prior to designing will also help designers feel assured throughout a design process, because creatives will feel confident whenever trying to achieve their initial intentions.

Also, the purpose of visualizing creative thoughts before designing is to aid creatives whenever trying to decide on certain ideas. Typically, most designers got through a phase where hesitation and uncertainty strikes. Usually, that state of being hesitant and uncertain will eventually affect a designer's ability to generate imaginative ideas. Naturally, creatives have the ability to develop creative ideas whenever inspiration strikes, though sometimes creatives feel unsure whether a particular idea might succeed or not, especially when a bunch of ideas surround a creative's brain. That moment specifically will require visualization and imagination of certain ideas and what such ideas might end up like. There will always be unexpected moments that will face designers at some point of their careers. Moments which might have a great impact on creations and outcomes, though it is all up to creatives whenever facing such obstacles.

To try and overcome such phases, creatives must understand that in order to succeed at a profession like design, creatives must think twice about attributes that affect creativity. Understanding that certain characteristics will eventually affect a designer's performance, yet realizing that in order to overcome such obstacles creatives must be more imaginative in order to produce innovative results. Becoming aware of such a theory will help creatives maintain original yet imaginative thinking with instant influences. After all, designers are creative individuals who are capable of achieving their desires. It is the way in which each creative chooses to accomplish a specific task that matters most. Thinking of a way which is guaranteed yet tested will without a doubt be helpful towards achieving individual goals set from the beginning of a design process.

Surely there are many ways designers can think of to be inspired. Since inspirations are known to be effective for creatives, there will always be the need to pursue such feelings and sudden thoughts. By being imaginative, creatives must express their creative skills which have originally emerged from initial inspirations. Every creative differs completely from another, so the ways in which each individual tries to acquire such thoughts and feelings differ totally, though some basic objects which we are surrounded with might inspire anyone at any time, for instance, books, lying around shelves without anyone noticing any of the available yet reachable content that actually needs attention. No ever thinks about what books might offer nowadays, especially in an ever-evolving technological industry which basically eliminates knowledge. Becoming more aware of books and what might they offer will help individuals realise that thoughtful information exists only in books, where the voice of an author is heard.

Surely, books are considered as inanimate objects, though whatever books contain should be regarded as valuable content which has been expressed by none other than a writer. It is the effort of each individual that matters most, since the search for information from books requires personal effort to look into interesting subjects. Perceiving any information of sorts will lead individuals to different paths of thinking. Processing information obtained from books will then gradually lead individuals to generate ideas related to the same information perceived. Eventually, any sort of ideas or thoughts will develop into personal intentions or wishes which have been generated by the reader. Those certain thoughts and ideas will basically influence the receiver of information (in this case it is the reader), in order to feel inspired by any of the content already perceived. Inspiration strikes when the mind is clear yet surrounded by useful information, which clearly stimulates individuals to become productive by producing creative yet innovative results.

A process of such occurs only when individuals become inquisitive and intrigued about subjects of personal interest. Nowadays, book publishers publish books on all sorts of fields and subjects; mainly each publication house specialises in specific topics related to such fields. For creatives, books on design and visual communication are available in nearly all bookstores worldwide and online. Therefore, creative individuals should be encouraged by mentors and directors to spend more time around books. Being directed to do something beneficial will strengthen individual skills by expanding knowledge and awareness in a person. Expressing inquisitive characteristics will result in individuals who are intellectual and curious whilst always eager for knowledge. A profession like design will thrive, with such individuals representing a profession of such. Designers should never underestimate the power of knowledge at any stage of their careers. Facts and information should always be considered convenient ways which help inspire individuals to be more imaginative.

Knowledge gained from books will undoubtedly endure with creatives for a lifetime. Any information obtained will eventually be useful whenever researching for certain subjects at some point of a designer's career. Specific information will act like references and sources whenever being applied. The connection between knowledge and inspiration will force creatives to become imaginative individuals. Similar connections which also last a lifetime somehow exist. Experiences and certain moments are also connected in a way where specific moments cause individuals to become more mature, and wiser. That sort of connection will surely affect individuals positively because novice creatives are transformed into proficient creatives. Such a transformation is a result of a certain experience or a specific moment which creatives have previously encountered. Becoming aware that particular moments experienced by creatives might have an influence on personality will make creatives interact more often with other individuals. By interacting more often, such individuals will have an effect on one another. Whether topics discussed with one another are related to the design industry or not, it would not matter at this stage. For ideas to flow and gradually develop there must be a cause or force in which helps creatives trigger inspiration.

By bonding more often with other peers and discussing general topics, creatives will become more confident yet connected at the same time. No one can ever imagine the vast number of ways that help creatives attain inspiration. Each individual has their own ways, surely, but there will always be a time where creatives struggle to capture certain thoughts which inspire them to create. Taking a moment to realise that there is no need to chase inspiration, inspirations will instead follow you. Realizing that, as creatives, basics and fundamentals will matter at some point, though a slight moment or experience in time will have an effect forever. Such thinking will widen a creative's understanding towards the importance of interacting. Some individuals look up to others as role models or idols. In the creative industry, however, most creatives will have other creatives as their role models, or even wish to be mentored by particular creatives. It just shows how an industry like design is such an inspiring industry which keeps stimulating, motivating, encouraging, and even influencing individuals constantly.

There are also unexpected moments which may occur at times when creatives are not even prepared to begin discussions, or are just feeling apathetic. However, taking a moment to listen to what others have to say might be rewarding at times. Respecting other individuals and their views will help perceivers realise other subjects they are not actually aware of. Therefore, listening to other perspectives will not only broaden a creative's understanding, but transform thinking abilities from an individual as well. Expanding comprehension abilities will aid creatives whenever generating ideas. The purpose of gaining information from other individuals with greater experience is to help creatives evolve unconventional ideas. By thinking unconventionally, creatives become able to transform existing ideas into imaginative intentions of their own. Truly, each individual is unique in their own way; it is all about individual efforts and determination, after all. Imaginative thinking requires certain standards achieved by nothing other than a strong desire. Expressing creative skills on a constant level will require a suitable surrounding. Being surrounded by experienced peers and individuals will be useful.

Some individuals are able to have an effect on others and some just are not able to. It all depends on the experience levels each individual obtains. Any sort of influence on other creatives will without a doubt be of an individual's own benefit. Learning from none other than experienced individuals will help novice creatives become more aware of their profession. Most importantly, experienced creatives will have a marked effect on such creatives which will last forever. Such an impact will help creatives develop imaginative ideas which have been originally transformed from initial ideas. Experienced creatives should always be seen as mentors and advisors who should be respected for their achievements, without whom an industry like design would not be able to flourish.

Inspirations should be regarded as surrounded feelings which stimulate creatives to become imaginative, accessible in many different ways although totally controlled by creative individuals solely. The purpose of being inspired matters greatly, because without any eagerness, creatives would not be able to generate original ideas which eventually evolve into creative solutions. Creatives may be inspired by unexpected moments or objects or even specific people. Each individual is distinctive in their own way, and should never be judged on personal views. Some common examples might inspire creatives instantly, like information recognised from books or specific experiences from special moments. It all depends on how each individual deals with or faces such incidents which basically encourage creatives to become more inventive.

An influence, on the other hand, is seen as a marked effect on a character. Such an impact on a specific individual is regarded as an influence. Some influences could cause an inspiration, at times. A change in a process or behaviour is most likely the result of an influence on a character. That sort of influence will eventually have an effect on personal feelings, which will then result in an inspiration caused by an influence. For designers to experience such influences in order to be inspired, interaction will be a key figure. Communication and involvement with other peers will give creatives a different perspective on different fields. Creativity will only function with imaginative ideas. Therefore, creatives should always try their best to obtain any inspirations and influences from their surroundings. Without such effects on creative souls, the process to gradually develop creative ideas will most certainly face obstacles along the way. Imaginative creatives will always need to be inspired and affected in order to achieve an objective. Developing thinking skills in an imaginative way will lead to constant creativity. As designers, persistent creative ideas will shape a complete design, which will eventually turn out to be successful yet effective towards others at the same time.

For designers, what actually matters most is the final result. However, the purpose of getting to a final solution is to find a resolution which has to be effective and influential. The process to achieve such a result would not be easy, surely. Without imaginative thinking, designers will fail to achieve an effective result. Understanding that the purpose of designing and creating is more than just about visual appearance and satisfaction. Realizing that the reason to produce and develop such influential results will be prominent towards the function of certain communities and societies. By becoming aware of such significance, creatives will realise the importance of producing effective results on a regular basis. An industry like design will continue to flourish rapidly with imaginative minds leading the way forward. Without imaginative results, designers would not be able to satisfy clients before satisfying themselves. Designers as creative individuals are never pleased with results which lack the approval of their creative souls. For imaginative individuals, this sort of feeling is considered normal and typical for such personalities. Displaying eagerness attributes will help designers develop creative thinking skills in order to be productive. Expressing enthusiasm by having the intended desire to achieve such influential results will transform individual abilities in a designer. Trying to be affected and influenced from certain surroundings will benefit the generation of creative ideas. Without creativity, designers will certainly lack producing imaginative results, which is normally caused by effects surrounding a designer.

# Chapter 10
## Design Management

Most creatives dismiss the idea of further developing a career like design. A profession of such creative calibre can sometimes distract a creative's focus by solely focusing on creative content. An industry like design should consist of individuals with a managerial background in order to support members of a design team to further develop strategic thinking. By directing and leading other creatives to achieve certain goals, an effective environment will gradually unfold. Having guidance and direction around a creative environment will also help individuals enhance their abilities while maintaining effective results. Design management is considered the business aspect of design, identified as a business discipline which mainly deals with developing, achieving, and managing an effective creative system. The purpose of design management is to assist other creatives with strategizing and planning, while implementing leadership skills in order to achieve certain goals.

Considering a managerial education as a design graduate will benefit creatives who are willing to pursue a career in design agencies or brand companies, though a degree in design management would not be necessary for all creatives who plan on developing individual skills as creative individuals. Since managerial roles are meant for a higher hierarchy creative, most designers would not feel the need to look into such a subject.

However, having a slight background on design

management will be necessary for all creatives who practice design on a daily basis. Becoming aware of the purpose of management in design will help creatives understand the business field related to the process of achieving goals for an income. Knowing how to manage an efficient yet effective system will be crucial for creatives whenever trying to achieve client needs. Understanding the basics of design management will help creatives develop individual skills which could impact their own performances. One of the main reasons to develop such effective skills is the impact such skills might have on a character. Developing an understanding in such a field will naturally cause leadership skills to unfold in a natural way. For creative professionals, displaying leadership skills regularly in a creative environment will be necessary in order to succeed at design management.

Design is an industry that depends very much on strategy. Without a specific strategy, designers would not be able to achieve certain goals. Strategizing is regarded as an art, where planning and directing collide with one another to form an effective process which is basically known as the design process. Every design team has their own ways of achieving such goals, though how each team strategizes is seen as the art aspect of a strategy. Creative ways and techniques differ from one individual to another. Therefore, the problem a creative individual faces will be solved differently as well. More often, planning and directing roles are handed to creative directors, though most creative directors fail to achieve successful results after strategizing, for some such situations would not matter at all, however some individuals just lack particular skills which become useful in such moments. It does not matter what position a creative individual is in to implement such skills.

What actually matters most is the preparations which occur before such moments. Preparing oneself with useful information will gradually develop an individual's understanding of such experiences. Aligning a strategy is one of the key roles for design management. Without an initial plan before designing, the outcome basically would not end up as successful as thought to be. Before beginning a design process, creatives begin strategizing in an efficient manner. That process of looking for an appropriate solution occurs for design management roles as well. The only difference is that designers strategize to find a temporary solution, whereas design managers are responsible for permanent strategizing which affects a whole team. Short-term strategizing is all about planning for a specific period of time, which is normally experienced upon receiving a design brief. However, long-term strategizing is totally regarded as the next level.

A higher level of performance is essential without a doubt, though qualifications and abilities will surely matter greatly as well. Being responsible for planning a process to achieve an aim, which matters for a certain group of people, will pretty much result in controlling individuals. Having the authority and control to decide on a strategy will definitely have an effect on any outcome. Such individuals will eventually influence team members by directing and guiding their behaviour upon achieving required results. Having the power of controlling a creative environment is pretty tough indeed, though having individuals with certain abilities will surely benefit other members trying to achieve specific goals. The whole purpose of having a strategy prior to designing is easing the process of achieving required results. Having a certain approach will help designers accomplish a design process without any complications or obstacles. Constant practice will greatly aid creatives to develop experience such a crucial field demands for. Having an evident strategy throughout a design process will be necessary and extremely essential whenever managing design related outcomes. Competent creative individuals will continue to inspire other designers whenever displaying managerial attributes. After all, becoming an individual who is able to think of a strategy is most likely to succeed at managing in a design environment.

Another key role for design management is managing the quality of design outcomes while enhancing user experience by creating new solutions. By demonstrating managerial skills in an efficient way, the quality produced becomes much more thoughtful and successful. Simple yet so effective skills surround the managerial concept, which every creative should look into. Planning, decision-making, communication, problem-solving, and motivation are all aspects of design management. Implementing such skills requires understanding and knowledge of a field of such significance. Becoming aware of management skills will increase productivity by establishing an effective system. For creatives, such skills are vital to further developing leadership skills. Whenever planning or strategizing, creatives are normally developing a concept. Gradually, decision-making evolves and decisions are made to proceed with the design process. Communicating with other peers will be ongoing to direct and achieve specific needs. By accomplishing a certain goal, a solution for a problem is delivered. Motivating creative peers will eventually lead to successful results along the way. Such an active process requires an individual who leads by example, someone who is able to control an environment which deals with creativity and communication combined.

Only results and solutions will reveal the success of a design manager. To be able to manage the quality of a design outcome requires individuals who act like passionate leaders, basically. Especially in an industry like design, leaders without a creative background would not be able to succeed at design management. Therefore, no matter what position a creative individual is in, improving individual skills will be vital for further career developments. Being able to manage a design process should be considered an evaluation by creatives. Testing personal abilities will develop strength and confidence in a character. For creatives, succeeding at maintaining such managerial skills will eventually be useful in enhancing an individual's character as a designer. Observing the process designers go through to achieve certain goals is also part of design management. Making sure that the quality of design being produced is sufficient enough to meet a client's need will reveal individual strengths at achieving particular tasks.

Any creation produced by designers should be presented with high standards. Evaluating the quality of an outcome requires sharp eyes and professionalism. Revising and examining any result before being presented will give creatives the chance for further enhancements and adjustments. Adjusting is also regarded as part of decision making, which should be active whenever managing a design. Aspects of such will lead creatives whenever implementing managerial skills. Taking a moment to carefully understand such aspects will result in successful design management. Developing certain skills with even further understanding will improve individual performances gradually. Experiencing managerial skills will certainly help creatives achieve unconventional solutions, which will greatly influence users and consumers alike. Such an effect on others will totally rely on the impact of guidance and direction towards creatives in general.

Having a leader amongst creatives is as important as having creatives who create visually communicative work to accomplish such tasks. Without guidance and direction, creatives will certainly feel lost. Having a leader who successfully implements leadership skills towards others will lead creatives to achieve further enhanced solutions. Someone who leads by example is someone who is well aware of leadership skills; an individual who is able to lead, direct, and manage other individuals while helping creatives reveal the best possible solution they could achieve. Such attributes are of true leaders who inspire others to create and become imaginative. Leadership skills consist of specific skills which transform individual abilities to become more responsible for a certain category. Maintaining leadership skills will help individuals achieve managerial attributes. For creative individuals, understanding that design management would not be successful without implementing leadership skills will be crucial for creatives who wish to develop individual abilities.

Like all professions, design would not thrive or flourish without leaders who manage day to day achievements. Developing communication skills will enable creatives with greater confidence whenever participating or getting involved in discussions amongst others. Cooperating with other creatives, for example, will strengthen communication skills by assisting creatives to collaborate with one another. Analysing solutions before being presented will help creatives evaluate an outcome while providing feedback at the same time, which will most certainly end up becoming useful towards the final outcome that has been presented. Stating a response by reacting in a professional manner will help improve anything being achieved by creatives. It is important to keep in mind that communication and feedback are part of leadership skills that creatives should try and obtain over time. Inspiring one another especially in a creative industry will lead to passionate individuals who are eager to produce creative solutions. Having that sort of belief and trust is a result of effects from an influential leader, not to forget that motivation is also regarded as a part of leadership skills, which would not be achievable without influencing behaviour in a particular way.

Spreading motivation amongst creative peers will establish a more cheerful and optimistic environment. Leaders who express motivational words to other team members are most likely to have spread influential words, which will affect behaviour and productions in a more positive way. For an industry like design, having motivational leaders with a prominent managerial role will surely be beneficial towards a whole team. By motivating other creatives, results will end up being more effective, since any successful result will depend on the effect of guidance on creatives. Becoming aware of such skills will broaden a creative's understanding. Having creatives who are aware of guidance and direction will result in professionalism. Implementing leadership skills in a creative environment will inspire designers to achieve unconventional solutions. Influential leaders especially from a creative industry will aid productivity from creatives in a positive way. Having a design background before implementing leadership skills will aid performance levels and productivity from creatives. Basically, someone who is aware of the actual process that generates a creative system is someone who is most likely to succeed at achieving effective results.

Creatives especially need leaders who inspire them, by influencing one's character to create such effective solutions. Only with the right guidance and direction will creatives achieve such results from original intentions. Maintaining positivity and creativity in a creative environment will successfully lead to strategic thinking. Making sure that the environment which creatives are in is positive and bursting with creativity will eventually lead creatives to strategize and plan for what lies ahead. The design process gradually unfolds, and creatives begin to produce creative results while developing imaginative ideas. Having an individual who controls such steps will aid the whole process by making sure an aim is achieved. Objectives could not be achieved without a leader who guides and directs others. Managing a creative process requires individuals with certain abilities and characteristics. Creatives can develop certain skills which will end up becoming convenient at some stage. Therefore, having a desire to obtain such skills as creatives will greatly benefit the design industry.

Whether creatives work individually or in design agencies, becoming aware of worthy skills such as leadership skills will benefit an overall performance. Knowing how to handle certain situations or implementing professional skills will help creatives greatly whenever facing a design problem. It is important to realise that leadership skills are a set of skills obtainable by anyone. Such skills will instantly activate managerial attributes from an individual. Therefore, design management, for instance, would not be achievable without enabling such specific skills. Strategic thinking, communication, feedback, and motivation are all considered as vital aspects of leadership. Every single aspect is somehow related to have an influence on a particular character. Having any sort of influence on other individuals by inspiring such individuals to create and produce desired results is part of design management. By managing other peers or initiating a self-instructed process, creatives become in control of a development process.

Any outcome of sorts should turn out to be effective in order to become successful. Without an effective solution, the managerial process would basically result in failure, though with practice and experience, managers would eventually become more mature, thinking-wise. Constantly maintaining certain skills will result in more experienced individuals who are dependable. However, failing to achieve desired results, whether it is from clients or particular design briefs, will prevent creatives from further enhancing their skills. Listening to clients well or carefully understanding design briefs will help creatives manage a successful process which will end up resulting in satisfaction from both parties. Fulfilling one's desire by successfully producing an expected solution will raise expectations towards designers. Making sure that clients are satisfied with any outcome will lead to trust between both a designer and client. Such a relationship will build ties and connections between both segments.

Creativity and business are two different professions, though combining commerce and design will cause commercial projects to develop more frequently. For a creative industry like design, frequency is quite important for the development of the creative sector. With constant activity, production levels would raise which will one way or another support the creative industry financially. Supporting designers by constantly keeping them active will massively impact the industry as a whole. Getting to that level of success surely requires commitment;

creatives should dedicate themselves to achieving pleasing results. Satisfying clients will lead to gaining connections more frequently, which will eventually strengthen an individual's reputation. Forming such ties and connections with a corporate sector will form an ongoing business which will most likely increase an income by receiving a profit. Such worthy benefits would not be attainable without particular individuals who control similar success. It is important for creative individuals to understand that without achieving an intended aim successfully, advantages would not be accessible at all.

Having creatives who are able to manage a creative process around or within a group of creatives will greatly affect any outcome of sorts. Managing a creative process successfully will depend on implementing leadership skills. Becoming able to guide and direct other creatives into achieving objectives is considered as the mission which will be facing any design manager. Delivering a successful solution along the way is part of a creative process, though making sure that any solution turns out as expected while still satisfying a client, will reveal how successful the design manager was at achieving an aim while still delivering an outcome. Accomplishing such a task will strengthen creatives mentally while gaining further experience at the same time. Creatives who are willing to learn will develop particular skills gradually. With constant practice performance levels would end up becoming more professional, which will greatly affect creatives. An industry like design is regarded as a creative industry. People normally disregard the fact that such an industry functions like most other industries. The creative world is not just about implementing artistic techniques. However, it should be perceived as an effective system; most just ignore such importance. Representing the creative industry appropriately requires creatives to develop personal skills in order to be noticed and regarded. Leadership skills are most certainly influential in every aspect. Transforming personal skills will require patience and understanding from creatives. As designers, such influential skills will always be obtainable to further enhance creative qualities.

An influential leader will clearly be noticed amongst other individuals. Becoming able to inspire designers to create while directing in order to achieve certain goals will clearly define a passionate leader. For the creative industry, having creatives transform individual skills to become more influential towards others will result in dominant creatives. Evolving to become distinguished amongst others, creatives will affect performance levels from other individuals. Therefore, having an impact on other individuals requires instant influence. Basically, any sort of effect on a character or behaviour will be the result of an influence. Surely the advantage of obtaining particular skills which could influence others is remarkable. Becoming a part of another individual's success will be great to witness absolutely. For designers especially, becoming part of an accomplishment will greatly motivate creative souls. By bonding with one another creatives become more confident of their abilities. Strengthening confidence will eventually reveal professional attributes from an individual. Therefore, becoming aware of design management will benefit creatives greatly by revealing distinguished features from creative characters.

Designers should be recognised for their performances and profession amongst others. Only by revealing a dominant character will creatives be noticed and respected. Design management is one way to achieve such recognition which all creatives should be acquainted with. Representing the design industry with clear managerial attributes will right away give a special impression. A notable sense will be perceived from a different point of view. Such an impeccable perspective will only be attainable with certain attributes. Creative individuals should always represent their profession in the best possible way. A designer is more than just a creative; a designer is someone who provides all sorts of effective solutions which visually communicates to satisfy people's needs. Obtaining particular features will certainly strengthen creatives to become professional individuals. Without a positive impression, creatives would always end up being underestimated by any opposition.

# Chapter 11
## Design and Culture

Values and tradition represent an individual's identity; following certain principles and living in a specific way reveals a particular culture every individual belongs to. Culture is basically known as the way of life each individual lives in. Certain traditions, foods, beliefs, and architectural monuments are normally regarded as elements of a particular culture. Creative individuals as human beings belong to many different cultures around the world. Though, as creatives, most designers disregard their backgrounds in favour of current or temporary trends. Designers as creatives are known to produce appealing results which visually transforms into a way of communication. Incorporating cultural aspects into certain designs will express a designer's background by revealing particular touches and influences which represent a certain culture. Every individual has a personal background, an identity which represents an own way of living. Trying to implement part of cultural influences into creative productions will reveal the designer's identity while making other people aware of a new culture at the same time.

Combining culture and design will result in publicity which will make consumers feel even more intrigued to find out more about any interesting subject. Capturing someone's attention is always a tough task facing any designer. Therefore, creating solutions which tend to be curious towards consumers will help creatives achieve successful results. Designers as creative individuals should be aware of other cultures around the globe in order to get inspired more often. Many countries around the world contain artistic values and designs representing actual cultures.

For creatives, exploring certain sites filled with creative representations will most certainly benefit any process yet to be achieved. Looking for existing creativity from other cultures will be rewarding for creatives in many ways. Exploring anything related to design from other cultures around the world will instantly inspire creatives to create thoughtful solutions bursting with inventive ideas. Globally, cultures are known to have an impact on a whole nation, such influences not only affect individuals, though influences of such also affect organizations, societies, and industries alike. Becoming part of a culture basically translates to being influenced to follow certain ways which are known to everyone from a similar surrounding. Creatives should be aware of what other cultures have to offer in order to achieve globally acquainted solutions, which will eventually spread further awareness for perceivers in general. Exploring different cultures around the world will enlighten creatives while influencing individuals to produce exquisite results with more meaning, which will sooner or later satisfy the global market as a whole.

An industry like design is vital for many societies and organizations around the world. Visual communication helps direct people to accomplish day to day tasks. Designers are the individuals in charge of producing such solutions which aid communication in every aspect. Thinking of visual communication from a global perspective will make creatives realise that communication appears in many different languages which are meant to be recognised by certain people. Therefore, creatives should produce solutions which should clearly satisfy perceivers in order to ease the process of retrieving visual data and information. Language is also regarded as part of culture. People normally communicate in a specific language to understand one another.

As a result, presenting any communication visually requires research and study. Also, understanding how certain societies function will broaden a creative's thinking. Trying to satisfy particular perceivers from the same society will feel easy over time, though trying to challenge oneself by producing solutions which are able to satisfy perceivers from a multi-cultural background will certainly be demanding. Challenging individual abilities will strengthen creatives mentally. Producing creative solutions for multi-cultural societies requires enlightened creatives. Designers who explore different cultures around the world will easily feel inspired by what other cultures have to offer. Designers should explore more about different cultures around the world to further develop their understanding in visual communication from another perspective. Whether creatives decide to explore by travelling to different countries or just researching through books and visual content, it would not matter. What actually matters most is how willing a designer becomes to look into interesting cultures and gain knowledge.

Travelling, of course, will be much more adventurous than going through visual content, though whatever feels convenient will do the job just as well. The purpose of exploring other cultures gives creatives greater experience. Gaining knowledge and understanding by nothing other than exploring will enhance individual characteristics in a designer. Enlightened creatives will develop effective thinking skills constantly without complications along the way of any design process. Exploring other cultures also gives creatives the opportunity to explore and witness other ways of living. For designers especially, it will always be an advantage whenever exploring other cultures. Inspirations might strike at any moment in time whenever creatives perceive and take in new surroundings. Whether creatives are inspired by a specific monument or a particular pattern or even a random specific setting, it will all count as effective in many possible ways. Anything inspiring a creative individual will eventually end up being part of an outcome or creative solution. Such a marked influence on any result designers intend to produce will reveal innovative ideas implemented with original yet imaginative thoughts.

By implementing influences from other cultures to specific designs, creatives will feel the need to explore even more cultures that might be as inspiring. Creatives should think of exploring as a source of inspirational influences. Learning about other cultures by exploring influential sites or objects will greatly affect the way in which creatives process ideas. Another positive point of exploring cultures will be the satisfaction of the global market. Whenever creatives produce solutions with influences from other cultures for any brand, for instance, not only will such an outcome be successful locally, but globally as well. For example, anything recognised globally such as a particular food package or an advertisement for a certain product will result as being effective globally just as how it should attract an intended market. Trying to attract a global market requires an in-depth understanding of how different cultures retrieve visual communication. Adding influences from different cultures to a certain creative solution will satisfy a vast number of markets around the world.

Such influences may be anything, basically, from inspiring structures to floral motifs, Islamic patterns, or any simple inspiration from somewhere. Anything of such may be evolved and recreated into something visually attractive to capture the attention of perceivers. Designers as creatives have the ability to be inventive and develop imaginative solutions caused by inspirations. It all comes down to where and what has inspired such creatives. Focusing on inspirations before beginning any design process will be crucial in producing any successful solution. By looking for inspirations from other cultures, creatives will develop new ways of thinking while enabling creativity. Challenging oneself surely requires desire; as creatives nothing will be achievable without desire. Expressing will and desire will raise confidence in a character. With confidence, creatives will be able to explore various cultures with optimism. Hopefulness will be the key to finding inspirations from anywhere at any time. Such characteristics will be useful for designers whenever exploring other cultures in need for an inspiration to support any creative outcome.

Design is a term often used for decorative purposes or creations. Anything related to design is either creative or functional. For graphic designers specifically, any outcome of sorts should end up being as creative as possible, while spreading meaning through visually communicative elements that will eventually end up being functional. Becoming aware of the purpose of designing will alert creatives to take notice of similar creative yet functional results or creations being produced, or that have already been produced elsewhere. In order to direct one's attention elsewhere, creatives must be fully aware of anything yet to be faced or encountered. Before beginning to observe anything related to design, creatives must understand the history and background of any production. Many creatives neglect the fact that most cultures around the world have influences from designs as part of their identity. Cultures of such include a certain style, or creative production which is presented and displayed in an artistic way. For example, Mughal influenced motifs and styles laid on historic sites in India like the Amber Palace in Jaipur or the Red Fort in New Delhi are still being used for architectural purposes, food packaging, apparel, and so on…

Such an impact shows how artistic influences may spark creativity. Surely the Mughal Empire has left behind many other influential locations and sites to explore. To this day, Mughal arts and motifs have influenced creatives from all over the world. Also, the Mughal Empire was known for producing some of the highest level of craftsmanship in many artistic fields such as architecture, patterns, and jewellery making. Part of India and Pakistan today consider Mughal art as part of their culture, which continues to inspire creatives and artists today. By becoming aware of such influential creations, creatives will continue to develop their understanding of other cultures while enlightening themselves. Becoming aware of other cultures will also act as a source of inspiration towards creatives. Not only will creatives benefit from such resources which are accessible in many ways, but most importantly creatives will gain consciousness of their surroundings which will greatly affect intentions and productions. Taking a moment to explore what other cultures have to offer from a creative perspective, will greatly influence designers to produce more imaginative ideas.

Many cultures around the world are recognised by decorative influences. Design could certainly be part of any culture, as long as certain communities continue implementing particular influences from a creative yet aesthetic area or object. Expressing appreciation and acknowledgement to anything in particular will raise admiration gradually. Such creative influences will only be part of a certain culture if communities recognise and acknowledge the existence of such productions. History also plays a major role with most cultures that have already been influenced from design. Without a doubt, histories of the past have shaped many cultures of today. Therefore, decorative monuments and creations from the past should always be cherished, in order to continue influencing generations yet to come.

Unfortunately, some societies today lack preserving such sites and masterpieces which is a concerning matter for most. Officials should try their best and maintain historic sites with great influences. Maintaining any part of history will eventually continue to spread awareness towards perceivers. Recognition will soon follow, and so history becomes part of societies which clearly reveals a 'culture' or a way of living, influenced from the past. By protecting the past, cultures become preserved. Doing so will support the formation of an identity which will be based on nothing other than a particular culture. As creatives, designers should always be influenced from their own culture first before looking for inspiration elsewhere. Being inspired by nothing other than someone's own culture will express the designer's identity whenever producing creative solutions.

Also, creatives will gradually develop a style of their own based on their culture. By developing a personal style, creatives will be able to express their personality. Without acknowledging a personal culture, creatives would never be able to understand other cultures. Recognizing the importance of someone's own culture will result in understanding individuals, who are appreciative of their own identity instead of negating it. Design will always be part of any culture as long as it remains acknowledged. It is vital for creatives to continue preserving their own culture in order for a certain culture to become noticed by others. Anything decorative or that has artistic value which becomes regarded by many others is naturally seen as part of a culture. Masterpieces of such should attract many global perceivers to eventually become known internationally. Such recognition and importance will always act as a source of inspiration for current creatives. Appreciating the existences of certain works will greatly benefit creative individuals, since creatives would not only become enlightened individuals, but compassionate intellectuals as well.

Producing creative solutions with global influences will have a great impact towards consumers on an international level. Creative individuals who are influenced from cultures around the world will be able to achieve outcomes that could satisfy perceivers globally. Implementing elements in a design with recognised aspects which have been recreated based on a designer's perspective, will express where certain influences have come from. Such expressions from an outcome will eventually reveal marked affects representing any particular design. Demonstrating creative elements through visually communicative results will help designers capture perceivers' attention instantly. Therefore, adding influences from different cultures will benefit designers by achieving an effective outcome. Creatives should try to imagine the functionality of certain cultures whenever designing. By discerning more about various cultures, designers will feel more motivated to recreate inspiring aspects which will eventually complete an intended design.

Encouraging oneself requires desire. Without wishing to accomplish a specific task or a particular aim, for instance, creatives would be directly led to failure. Positive individuals would basically achieve satisfying results without any complications. By finding out more about other cultures, designers would not only benefit from knowledge but confidence as well. Creatives who develop thinking skills from facts and information will be more confident whenever making a decision. Any process that involves important decisions will require self-assured individuals who are always confident. A design process, like many others, is also regarded as a process with significance. Creatives who are enlightened and informed by other cultures' facts and information, will be able to accomplish a design process with ease while providing useful yet creative details. Basically, the more enlightened creatives become, the more attention creatives will receive. Becoming able to produce work with familiar influences will primarily raise the expected target percentage.

Whenever designing, creatives should always be imaginative in order to achieve effective solutions. Developing creative ideas with cultural influences will help creatives achieve successful results which will please many categories and groups. The main purpose of visual communication is to direct people while expressing meaning with a visually appealing language. Generally, the meaning of particular languages is entirely part of semantics. For creatives, understanding that creative solutions of all sorts should portray a visual message which expresses meaning is vital. Basically, creative solutions depend on meaning from languages, which is known as semantics. Without presenting a meaningful message, which depicts a language that is initially targeted for a certain group, creatives would be unsuccessful at capturing a desired attention. Producing work which eventually becomes noticed by others will gradually be part of a specific culture.

Any result which affects behaviour by any means will have the possibility to affect the whole society. Recognised creative solutions will never be considered an easy achievement by creatives. Having a creative production which receives any sort of appreciation from an entire society will be very pleasing and fulfilling for creatives, surely. Such an achievement will gradually become part of a society because of confessing its importance and existence. Whether creatives produce certain signs or come up with an appealing advertisement, as long as any result ends up being effective, creatives will have the chance to be recognised. Once a whole society has approved of such a production, the effect will be clearly noticed. Gradually, societies and communities become guided by visual communication which naturally begins to affect a person's behaviour. Any production with visually communicative content will be regarded as a creative solution which is entirely intended to have an effect. Trying to achieve a global affect requires creatives to become more inquisitive. Becoming interested in learning more about other cultures will support creatives massively. Therefore, creative individuals should always be curious and eager to learn about information they are not aware of. With awareness and perception of certain cultures, creatives would be able to achieve global marketing recognition by implementing familiar elements which tend to be effective towards others.

Adding cultural influences to any design will always end up being beneficial. Such an advantage will help creatives achieve satisfying results constantly. Design and culture are both regarded as terms situated within function. Certain cultures function with creative elements and ways of perception while most designs are initially created to become partly effective. Also, certain cultures depend on particular designs, whether they are concerned with visual communication or architecture, or even recognised styles; anything basically part of culture which is known to have creative and artistic value could support the function of certain societies, communities, and organizations. Creatives may look at different cultures as part of an inspiration or just to learn something new. Either way, as creatives, designers are able to develop ideas influenced from particular surroundings to support any production or creative solution. Therefore, it doesn't actually matter if creatives decide to explore certain cultures as part of gaining knowledge, because any information gained will eventually have an effect on creatives at some point.

Enlightening oneself requires a great amount of effort, especially if someone is to gain further knowledge and understanding of a specific subject. Designers who limit their understanding and knowledge will lack developing initial ideas that supports any creative process. Becoming aware of worthy topics and certain cultures, for example, will greatly impact creative individuals in many ways. Such a significant effect will be clearly noticed in the quality of work being produced by designers. Designs which have been produced with extra thought and understanding will eventually look well executed. Such results will always express professionalism, which every designer should try to attain. Professional results will reveal more about the designer in charge of achieving such a compelling outcome. Gradually, creatives will begin to develop confidence whenever supporting any outcome from all the knowledge already secured prior to designing. With knowledge, creatives will always feel informed and aware. Especially for an industry like design, without information, obtained ideas would never evolve to support creatives during a process. Every creative outcome depends on an initial idea. Therefore, creatives should always enlighten themselves to have actual support from facts and information, which will continue to influence any creative production yet to be developed.

Creative individuals have the ability to generate ideas based on certain influences to support any creative outcome. Most creatives dismiss the fact that research actually assists such a process. Influences are basically available anywhere at any time. Surely it is up to creatives to reveal their efforts and begin to investigate with desire. By doing so, creatives will be able to broaden thinking skills while obtaining knowledge from certain surroundings. Also, creatives may not realise that they are already surrounded by different cultures. Such cultures may be the key to influencing creatives to become innovative individuals. Becoming aware of one's surroundings will unfold many solutions creatives may be after. The power of culture on designers will be very dominant. An influence of such impact on creative souls will help creatives achieve more meaningful results with professional attributes. Also, creatives will be able to develop a certain style or identity based on a specific culture. While implementing influences from other cultures, creatives will gradually become recognised for the styles being developed. Designers may be acknowledged for creative solutions that relate to certain cultures based on style. With such an apparent recognition an identity based on inspirational environments becomes evident towards perceivers.

Designers should always realise the importance of certain

cultures in order to feel inspired and revitalised. Cultures exist for a reason, and designers as creatives should look for inspirations from cultures in order to continue developing imaginative work based on actual influences. By enlightening oneself, creatives will be able to achieve much more than what's usually expected. Gaining knowledge from other cultures by exploring ways of living and historic sites will surely result as valuable information being perceived. Since inspirations may strike at any moment in time, creatives will also feel inspired by particular surroundings which have been observed from the past. Any information gained by creatives will definitely be utilised at some stage of a creative process, with either a current or upcoming one. After all, creatives would not be able to function without inspirations, so exploring advanced subjects will greatly benefit creatives.

# Chapter 12
## Awareness from Visual Communication

Spreading visual communication by conveying meaningful messages in a form that can clearly be perceived is regarded as the main purpose of such an approach. Ideas and information merge with one another to produce visually communicative results. Such results are totally controlled and managed by none other than designers. Initial ideas are transformed and developed into creative solutions which are revealed at the end of a creative process. Generally, creative individuals become the ones in charge of producing such effective results, which should turn out to be influential in every aspect. Truly a process of such requires responsible individuals who are well informed. Developing any visual content requires skill and understanding in order to turn out to be successful while perceived. For any outcome to be as successful and effective, creatives must understand ways in which to attract a perceiver's attention. Any creative solution developed by designers should convey a message to an intended target.

Without understanding the fundamentals of design, creatives will not be able to achieve desired results. Visual communication is part of everyone's life without even noticing, which without its existence, people would feel lost and wouldn't be able to function. People basically rely on visual communication to communicate freely. Elements such as text, images, and shapes form visual solutions which are totally developed by creatives. Becoming aware of the importance of such effective productions will help creatives realise that a profession of such is demanded and required amongst communities and societies alike. Whenever perceiving any visual content, people normally become aware or conscious of a particular message, which will eventually help perceivers realise and understand the initial intention set by designers.

Messages of such are demonstrated and set visually to attract attention so that perceivers become aware of anything conveyed. That specific connection between a designer and a perceiver is pretty vital, because the success of any outcome depends solely on perceivers reactions. Any result produced by creatives should have a direct impact towards both perceivers and consumers, as without a marked affect creatives would not be successful at all. An influence of such effectivity is most certainly required in the design industry. Making sure that each and every creative solution should have an impact towards others will retain attention from viewers, while helping creatives accomplish effective solutions. A profession like design is powerful enough to change how people think or react. Even so such effective solutions aim to direct and guide people to continue functioning freely every day. Relying on a profession like design will continue to encourage designers to keep achieving effective solutions all the time. Visual communication is considered an effective approach whenever processing information and spreading awareness, since people in general respond to visual content more easily by processing visually appealing solutions produced by creatives.

Facts state that the human brain responds to visual content much faster than written text. Studies also reveal that visual communication is the most effective way for people to perceive information. As a whole, visual communication relies totally on eyesight.

Different parts make up such a way for communication to be transmitted. Visual communication consists of graphic design, environmental design, typography, and film, most commonly, though other examples are also regarded as part of visual communication. What is important for creatives to understand is that the process of transmitting information through visual means and imagery matters greatly. Anything developed by creatives should somehow convey a message. The way ideas are presented towards an audience will reveal a creative's accomplishment. Without realizing the importance of producing influential results, creatives would never be able to impact perceivers. To have an impact on others, creatives must understand the fundamentals of design in order to implement innovative solutions. Without understanding the primary principles, creatives would not be able to achieve such effective solutions. An ever-evolving world requires creatives to produce imaginative solutions constantly. Today, no one can ever imagine living in a world without typefaces that are in everything an eye perceives. From sending text messages, reading a book or a magazine spread, medicine labels, and food packaging, typefaces are everywhere and no one can ever imagine living without their presence.

Mainly, typefaces and fonts are aspects of typography which are considered major design fundamentals amongst creatives. Typography as a field has evolved tremendously over the years. Ever since Johannes Gutenberg invented the printing press during the fifteenth century, movable type has evolved into what people recognise now as typefaces. Such a transformation reveals how visual communication can grow and develop over the years to support the transmission of information. Without creatives' effort and multiple attempts, such an evolution would not have existed today. Creatives need to be recognised and appreciated instead of ignored by perceivers. Disregarding the effort behind influential yet prominent creative solutions will prevent further enhancements yet to be discovered. Terminating creative development will greatly affect designers and expected productions.

Supporting the creative industry by becoming aware of how visual communication operates and functions will be crucial towards a creative's performance. Becoming aware of the importance of visual communication will also help creatives achieve effective results more frequently. Not only will creatives feel more responsible for any outcome, but as designers, creatives will gradually develop knowledge and understanding of such a matter, which will inspire creatives to frequently come up with even more imaginative solutions. Gaining an understanding of a subject like visual communication will always be beneficial for creative individuals. Understanding what sort of solutions work best or which type of result turns out as effective as it should be will aid any creative development process yet to come. Gradually developing creative ideas so that an outcome becomes easily perceived requires constant practice from designers. Without being active creatives would not be able to find a suitable solution which should spread awareness. Therefore, creatives should always be attempted to achieve an influential response, a reaction only perceivers and consumers are able to control.

Such an effect basically determines how successful a designer can or will be, though with the right attitude creatives will somehow find a way in which such an effect becomes clearly noticed.

Producing visually communicative solutions has many benefits towards perceivers, which every creative should be aware of. Processing information through visual forms requires creatives who are passionate and aware of their profession. Developing visual solutions which should transmit a message to a particular target requires research. For creatives, researching is also considered one of the fundamentals of design. Without investigating in depth about a particular design problem surrounding certain topics, creatives would not be able to achieve effective results. Becoming aware of detailed aspects surrounding a subject will raise curiosity levels from designers. Having that strong desire to find out a particular solution will greatly affect any outcome a designer develops. By looking into a specific subject during researching, creatives will gradually find a way to attract a perceiver's attention by coming up with an effective creative solution. An effective solution of such influence will have plenty of beneficial factors towards perceivers. Solutions produced by designers will not only appear creative, but communicative as well.

Spreading communication visually will result in information being simply transmitted. Processing visual communication is known to be much more convenient compared to other ways of communication. Perceivers will generally find visual content simple to process, since elements would be laid in an effective way instead of verbal or written communication, which are similar to old times. Also, visual communication is considered a successful approach because of how clear and straight forward information is presented. The way in which creatives implement certain elements to match grid systems expresses precise detailing from creatives. Visual hierarchy is known amongst designers as the arrangement of certain elements that should imply an influence towards perceivers upon facing a structured creative solution. Such an effect will influence the human eye in order to perceive the visual content presented. Colour and contrast, type, composition, and scaling are all part of the visual hierarchy process which every designer should go through precisely whenever designing. Without maintaining a visual balance from particular elements, solutions produced would not end up being as effective.

Designers become the individuals in charge of a design process. Therefore, taking the time to achieve an effective solution requires certain skills and understanding. Creatives who express knowledgeable attributes will be able to accomplish a design process without any complications. By developing creative solutions, designers gradually gain consciousness of reactions from consumers and perceivers. Becoming aware of such responses will specify if a creative solution turns out to be effective or not. Identifying the positives and negatives of any creative result will help creatives realise what needs to be adjusted for further enhancements towards creative productions yet to come. Creatives should always make sure that any result produced should be successful at producing an impact from an intended or desired initial wish. Basically, in order to achieve an effective solution, creatives must develop a result which has an impact. Creative solutions should have an influence towards perceivers one way or another. Without such an affect the message being portrayed visually would not be delivered.

A field with many benefits such as visual communication will always continue to attract interest from perceivers and consumers. Just realizing the ease of transmitting information through visually expressive solutions will make anyone appreciate the fact that such a way exists. Creatives deserve to be recognised for the effort displayed silently. Without creatives generating a very intricate process, visual communication would not be achievable or utilised. Realizing that an approach like visual communication is so expressive while continuing to increase awareness will not just enlighten creatives but perceivers as well. Relying so much on an approach of such makes people forget about the significance of such a field. Awareness is about the perception of knowledgeable facts and information. Without being able to perceive visually presented information, awareness would not be achievable or transmitted.

With visual communication, awareness will always be attainable. Perception of knowledgeable facts visually is the most effective way to process information. Spreading communication through visually communicative results is considered the most reliable way amongst perceivers. Therefore, creatives will always be the ones responsible for developing and producing solutions which attract attention. By achieving successful solutions, creatives will leave their marks and become a vital aspect of the link between information and awareness, a connection between creatives and perceivers that will remain hidden for some though widely influential for most. With a staple production or solution, creatives will be able to transform perceivers' reactions instantly. Continuing to develop such effective solutions will be the key for an influential response, which every creative individual should try and attain in order to be successful.

Every known profession has a mission which practitioners should follow in order to achieve certain goals. Visual communication in particular amongst every other profession has a demanding sort of mission which is important in every aspect. Every designer understands that the purpose of producing creative solutions is to transmit a visual message. The goal of achieving such effective solutions is to portray visually communicative results which convey meaning and understanding to perceivers. Without maintaining such results, creatives would not be able to become successful individuals. Creative solutions produced by designers are carefully generated with the intention of having an impact on perceivers. Developing such solutions are intended to guide and direct people to function everyday of their lives.

Surely it is interesting for creatives to witness such responsive results from perceivers, especially if such results are personally produced. Creative solutions are known to have a marked effect on perceivers in many ways. The influence between a creative result and a perceiver or consumer is clearly noticed. Whether it is an advertising campaign trying to attract buyers or certain signs and symbols directing perceivers to continue their ways, every creative solution developed by creatives will result as influential one way or another. Eventually, the communication portrayed by visual forms becomes the effective factor. By coming up with results which are meant to transmit a message, creatives become the link between information and perceivers. Also, creatives are responsible for attracting attention from perceivers while generating an effective creative solution. Visual forms of communication can be any element a designer includes in a creative solution which tends to portray a visual message. Elements such as type, shape, and colour are all regarded as part of creative solution which a designer develops during a design process.

A design process is basically regarded as an experimental phase amongst designers. Without developing initial ideas further, creatives would not be able to achieve such influential results. By exploring certain ways and techniques creatives will eventually discover the appropriate solution to convey a message. Attracting a perceiver's attention requires experimentation by creatives. Without trying new ideas and implementing various elements, creatives will not be able to visualise a concept which will act as the source behind a creative solution. Developing an effective solution requires effort from designers. Without determination, creatives will never be able to accomplish influential results. Any result of such influence should be displayed to spread awareness while addressing perceivers to react in a specific way. Exposed attraction is what all designers should aim to achieve, since any displayed or presented outcome should tempt perceivers in the most creative way best possible.

Creative productions are exposed in many different forms to the public. Perceivers do not actually notice that they are being guided through such forms until a visual message is depicted, only then will perceivers notice that anything perceived will begin to raise an individual's awareness. An awareness so vital which without no one can ever communicate. Visual forms of communication have been present since the ancient ages, though such forms have been greatly evolved into what we work and perceive nowadays. Just imagining that computers and digital media did not exist back in the old times will make anyone wonder how communication was portrayed back then. Truly, there are many classifications of computers, since the first production in 1822 by Charles Babbage.

However, the initial creation does not actually resemble a modern-day computer which everyone is aware of. Personal computers were first introduced in the 1970s, which aided the process of visual communication being digitally produced and developed. Before that, everything creatives worked with was developed with extra effort and time, since most of the work was hand drawn. Creatives back then had to go through a much-complicated process compared to designers nowadays, since available programmes makes the design process achievable much quicker. Thinking of the ancient ages, some of the earliest forms of visual communication did actually exist during the Pharaohs period. Mainly, ancient Egyptians communicated through visual forms which are considered to be very intricate. Such forms are displayed in all over the historic sites of Egypt today. During that period of time, the Pharaohs mostly communicated through writings and hieroglyphics. Ancient Egyptians or the Pharaohs also used drawings and pictures to express moments of their lives.

Without the presence of such forms, historians would not be able to analyse and study ancient periods. Portraying messages through visual forms will always be considered an expressive approach, especially with proof from ancient ages such as the period of the Pharaohs, and their way of visual communication. Any sort of visually communicative form will continue to convey some sort of meaning which expresses a message. Depicting messages through visual forms will always be considered an influential process, just like it did in the past. Such influence will not only affect people for a specific period of time; instead, such influential solutions will have a permanent affect. Also, visual communication is able to instantly influence cultures by becoming a recognised part of certain societies and communities whenever creative solutions appear widely. Again, just like ancient Egypt, the Pharaohs expressed and revealed how they lived through visual forms.

Egyptians nowadays still have some of the Pharaohs' influences used in their culture. Certain clothes and jewellery represented during the Pharaohs' period are still produced in Egypt today. Without expressing moments of their lives, the Pharaohs would not have revealed their period of time. No one would ever come to know about their traditions and ways of life, which most Egyptians today recognise as part of their culture. Various images of foods, for instance, are depicted in burial chambers. Such foods are, to this day, used as part of the Egyptian cuisine known by every citizen. Influences of such great impact will continue to live on for generations and generations yet to come. As creatives, designers should always try to implement influences from the past in order to achieve an effective response. By being more expressive while coming up with creative solutions, designers will be able to attract attention instantly. Looking for inspiring examples will greatly influence any outcome yet to be achieved by creatives. With a knowledgeable background, creatives will always be well informed and prepared to produce effective solutions all the time.

Creatives are meant to come up with visually communicative results which portray meaningful messages. Surely with facts and information, creatives would be able to support any expected development process which requires such effective solutions. Clearly looking for particular resources and references will aid the generation of ideas in order for creatives to develop influential results. Designers should always keep in mind that any final outcome should be clear and straightforward in order to result in an effective solution. Any creative solution designers develop should convey a meaningful message that is easily perceived. In order for creative solutions to be successful, the perception process should be attractive and tempting at the same time. Creatives should be aware of certain ways to capture a perceiver's attention. The overall appearance of a creative solution is one way to judge the success of an outcome which is yet to be noticed. By analysing an outcome, creatives begin to understand what sort of elements attract perceivers and which do not. This sort of decision-making skill will greatly benefit creatives by raising confidence levels.

Designers will gradually realise useful ways and ideas which will eventually affect any outcome while implementing influential results. Also, creatives will gradually learn more about a perceiver's way of discerning visual communication. With constant practice, creatives will be able to find a solution faster than expected. Capturing a perceiver's attention requires a complete understanding of such a matter. Becoming aware that the development process is vital towards the outcome will make creatives consider the idea of further developing and enhancing any creation so that it impacts an intended target. Transmitting communication through visual forms will always be considered to be a tough task facing any designer. Definitely, the responsibility a creative individual faces is pretty serious. Every solution a creative produces should express meaning in order for perceivers to be aware of the message being portrayed. Visual communication will continue to influence perceivers from various societies and backgrounds as long as creatives become successful at achieving such effective results.

Certainly, without developing influential solutions, communication would not be visually expressed. Therefore, creatives should always reveal their capabilities in the best possible way. By maintaining such effective results with great impact, creatives will become consequential individuals, who will always be considered vital figures every community needs in order to develop visually communicative results. Creatives should always aspire to become an essential part of any community. By displaying vital, effective solutions which reveal awareness to the public, creatives will become required more often. Such effects will make perceivers attracted to creatives and their productions. Any successful connection between perceivers and creatives will result in increased productivity, which will leave designers more engaged. Being commissioned constantly is a positive sign for every creative individual. Constant activity will help creatives become more productive while improving the quality of upcoming productions. Without being expressive, creatives will not gain attention from perceivers. Distinguished creative individuals will be eminent amongst others, while continually leaving a notable impression behind them.

As an approach, visual communication will always be considered influential. Whether it is creatives, perceivers, or consumers, everyone agrees that a field of such significance is vital for all. The way visual communication affects certain people makes it a more controlled approach. Creatives actually become in charge of limiting such influences from initial intentions. An impact of such becomes restrained by creatives who actually decide who their actual target is. When it comes to identifying a target group, creatives begin a development process in which effective solutions become gradually completed. Every designer's mission is to produce visually appealing solutions which have to communicate a certain message. Achieving an aim of such will identify how successful a designer turns out to be. Creatives should always attempt to be more thoughtful whenever generating ideas which shape a final outcome. By revealing more thought and consideration, ideas become more musing.

With such thoughtful ideas, creatives will be able produce imaginative solutions all the time. Such minor details will greatly reflect an expected outcome once completed. Especially with visual communication, solutions without imaginative ideas behind them would not be as effective as they should. Supporting a creative outcome with innovative ideas would give designers an opportunity to be even more creative. Visual communication will continue to evolve successfully only if creative minds become more responsible and considerate. Showing careful thought while developing creative solutions will benefit everyone related to the creative industry. Also, visual communication will continue to affect others only if creative solutions become more reliable. Therefore, as creatives, designers should be well prepared to face any design problem requiring a creative's effort. Also, creatives should continue to develop individual skills in order to satisfy the public. Providing the creative industry with influential solutions will greatly benefit the evolution process. As an industry, design depends on the reaction of people. Continuing to entice perceivers will be the key for any success yet to come. With visual communication, tempting will surely be possible in many ways which only a creative will be aware of. With knowledge and understanding, creatives will be able to produce effective solutions that will help the creative industry to flourish.

# Chapter 13
## Visual Communication Towards Consumers

Visual Communication has been influencing many generations of the past and present ever since it first evolved in the fifteenth century. To this day, visual communication is known to have an impact on every living soul depending on such an effective approach. To many individuals, visual communication will just be a typical approach, though to wise individuals, visual communication will always be recognised as a vital aspect. Realizing that an approach like visual communication is more than just a way of communicating will help raise awareness levels in perceivers and consumers alike. An approach for such an impact should be seen as an effective yet persuasive approach, where creative solutions become in control to help people function everyday of their lives. Users, consumers, and perceivers are all affected by visually communicative results whether it is actually noticed or not. Such a marked effect will reveal how a creative solution turns out to be. Without producing successful results designers would not be able to have an impact on a specific target. Creatives should always try to achieve persuasive results which eventually tempts the viewer or perceiver.

Innovative ideas developed by designers can always attract attention from perceivers. Solutions which express creativity in every manner will continue to result in success every time they are presented or displayed. Failing to achieve such imaginative solutions will never benefit creative individuals. Trying to balance creativity with understanding will help creatives produce influential solutions without any complications. By understanding what needs attention, creatives will be able to identify creative solutions that best suit a problem of such. Without identifying a cause for a design that expresses visual communication, effective outcomes will be hard to achieve. Consumers react in many different ways whenever exposed to visually communicative results. Some consumers become easily attracted by creative solutions, while some consumers do not pay attention at all to such creative details which might have an influence. Either way, consumers and perceivers of all types are being directed by visually constructed designs which spread communication.

Designers as creative individuals are solely responsible for coming up with such effective solutions. In order to accomplish persuasive solutions, creatives must be aware of who their actual target is. Reactions to products, advertisements, or signs will differ from one individual to another, though producing creative solutions with extra thought and understanding will be the key to success. Capturing a perceiver's attention requires more than just certain skills. Gaining experience gradually will benefit creatives whenever generating ideas and producing such effective solutions. Becoming aware of how perceivers react to visual content from a scientific perspective will greatly benefit designers as well. Slight details may not be noticed upon completing a design, though without noting such vital details, outcomes will not be achieved as expected. Paying attention to slight details during any design process will always be necessary for designers. Considering aspects which might affect a creative production whenever designing will help strengthen confidence in a designer. Also, experience will be gained at the same time. Reinforcing individual abilities will help creatives achieve more than they could expect. Especially in a field like visual communication, where creativity aids the transmission of visual messages. An approach of such significance will always continue to impact and attract perceivers by the production of visual content which communicates in every aspect.

Over the years, visual communication has evolved tremendously while continuing to influence consumers at the same time. The purpose of producing such effective results is for consumers to be able and to accomplish personal tasks. Whether it is part of a specific job or just an individual matter, consumers react to visual content in different ways that best suits their roles. A modern-day consumer is regarded as someone who uses goods and services to satisfy individual needs. Consumers as well have progressed over the years. Therefore, creative productions have been developed and have transformed much more frequently compared to previous productions. Surely, much more demand is the reason for such occurring developments, since consumers back in the day did not have many choices to make whenever consuming products or deciding on selections. Nowadays, for instance, a dairy brand is not just seen as a provider of milk and dairy only, though consumers shop for dairy products based on ingredients and produce. Such facts allow other parties into the dairy business, which straight away results in competition. Products then begin to rival one another for sales and business purposes.

Initially, consumers are the ones to have led to such a system due to personal satisfaction. Products actually go through a long process before making it to the market, laid on shelves ready to be consumed. In order for any product to sell, appearance and presence will be a key figure. Designers become in charge of producing packaging lines that best suits each product. Back in the day, a yogurt pot would be very basic and straightforward, without any tempting elements. Nowadays, however, such a package would certainly not sell as it once did. Pleasing consumers is surely a difficult task facing any designer. Though with further understanding of such subjects that matter, creatives will be able to develop satisfying results regularly. Convincing consumers in a creative manner requires more than creativity.

Designers should study an issue of such importance carefully in order to come up with effective results. Without becoming aware of the actual target and their reactions, creatives will not be able to achieve convenient solutions. Today, consumers are very difficult to persuade compared to consumers from previous decades. Ever since technology has taken over everything consumers are surrounded with, the perception of visual communication has changed as well. Ways in which communication is visually expressed requires extra effort and numerous attempts in order to capture a consumer's attention. Certain styles, layouts, and colours are all considered and discussed carefully whenever designing. Consumers will always be tough individuals to persuade constantly because of the transformed thinking abilities each individual maintains over time. Therefore, prior to designing, creatives should research in depth about any project yet to be faced. By researching the history, purpose, function, and benefits of a particular yet expected product or brand, for example, creatives will gain further awareness of the subject itself prior to designing.

Also, by asking certain questions prior to designing,

creatives will obtain informative insights regarding creative solutions. Becoming aware of who the consumers are, or why consumers will need such a solution will greatly benefit creatives during any design process. Having an overall perception of consumers and their reactions before beginning to generate ideas will be crucial for creatives whenever coming up with an effective solution, which initially tends to have an impact on consumers after being developed. Only with a deep understanding and lucrative background will creatives be able to find an appropriate solution which results in a successful reaction. Creatives should consider a process of such as an absolute advantage towards any production process. Surely consumers react in many different ways which are mostly unexpected; at times certain creations would have an instant response, while at times imaginative results would have an unusual reaction. Nothing is guaranteed in the design industry basically. Responses may at times be overwhelming, while also being surprising and unexpected at certain moments towards designers. What actually matters the most is having an influence on others while spreading meaning through visual forms.

With an impact of such, creatives will be motivated to generate further ideas which will most certainly turn out to be effective. Creative solutions based on experience will be more likely to result in a successful outcome. Whatever designers encounter throughout such a demanding profession like design, the mission in mind should always remain the same as always. Any solution waiting to be solved should express creativity while spreading meaning through visually attractive elements. With that in mind, creatives will be conscious of their primary purpose in producing such influential results. Valuing a mission of such impact, especially in an industry like design, will help guide creative individuals whenever developing designs to satisfy intended consumers.

Creatives somehow dismiss that consumers are regarded as perceivers in most cases. It is important to keep in mind that the word 'perceive' is derived from awareness and consciousness. In order for consumers to become aware of anything, basically, they will have to perceive any kind of information first of all. So, by perceiving visual forms which communicates in an expressive manner, consumers become able to distinguish and decide on personal needs. Perceiving information visually is a crucial part of visual communication. In order for any information to be perceived, visual content should appear to be clear and obtainable, making sure that anything presented conveys a meaningful message to the perceiver. Some creative solutions depend only on the perception of information rather than the consumption of products. For creatives, it is extremely vital to be aware of such a point. Since some solutions require very simple effort with slight features in order to be as effective, whereas consumer products require way extra time and effort in order for solutions to appear as tempting as possible.

Creatives should understand that perceivers and consumers are alike in many ways, though seen differently in some cases. However, creatives should always bear in mind that anything yet to be produced should always be effective in satisfying a desired target. Without a successful impact, creatives would not be able to please or persuade both consumers and perceivers. Understanding who the actual target will be, or how will such a creative solution become beneficial towards a certain criterion will greatly aid creatives whenever developing solutions. The purpose of developing such an influential result is for users to be able to function while being aware. Visual communication affects people of all sorts whether it is noticed or not. Such a vital approach should always be maintained by creatives in order to continue flourishing for the best. Signs and symbols for example fall under the subject of visual communication. A field which mainly deals with producing signs and symbols for direction purposes. Solutions developed from such a field rely on perception of visual messages only.

Perceivers who are visually directed from such results require simple arrangements that are very clear whenever perceived. Road signs, for instance, direct drivers to certain lanes in order to get to a preferred destination. Typefaces produced for such purposes should be easily perceived from a distance, because cars will be generating at a certain speed. Drivers in this case will be seen as the target whenever developing such solutions. Since car drivers will be considered as the perceivers in this case, creatives should understand and study how drivers react to signs and symbols before beginning a design process. Experimenting with layouts or testing various typefaces will be crucial at the development phase. Without such assurance and commitment creatives would not be able to achieve a convenient solution. Another example which relies on perception is airport signage.

Travellers go through many terminals to get to particular flights. Without symbols and signs distributed along terminals intended for guiding and directing travellers, airports would be a complete mess. Not a single traveller can imagine checking in at any airport without tilting and turning their heads, looking for signs. Typically, travellers will need to perceive signs in order to get to the departing gate. Such a case will have travellers as the primary target prior to designing. Creatives in such a case should be determined individuals who are well prepared.

Responsibility will be massive surely, therefore patience and diligence will be pivotal. Producing signs for a cause of such significance will require extreme clarity. Perceivers, in this case, will need precise signs which express what should be meant. Just like consumers, perceivers also require meaningful messages to be directed and guided to towards the right direction. Capturing attention requires more than just a basic layout.

To secure a perceiver's attention, creatives must be persuasive in every aspect. By obtaining someone's awareness, creatives become in control of linking meaning and communication. Also, by combining meaning and information, results would never lack expressiveness. Combining messages or information through visual forms will always be a tough task facing any designer. Therefore, understanding the purpose of such an approach will help creatives realise the importance of producing effective solutions which continue to have an influence on others. A term like perception in the design industry should be very well thought about whenever producing any creative solution. Creatives should always be aware of perceivers and consumers before making decisions that could have an overall effect. Carefully reviewing reactions and responses will make creatives wary of how consumers and perceivers interact with one another. Gradually developing skills and knowledge with constant practice will help creatives think of unconventional ways which will continue to have an impact on others. Perceivers, consumers, or users are all considered as human beings after all.

Accomplishing certain tasks to satisfy specific needs will be every designer's intention. Whether it is teachers, doctors, bankers, engineers, or chefs, any existing profession basically relies on visual communication one way or another. Believing it or not would not support creatives to function, though appreciating an approach of such significance and importance will greatly affect creatives.

Attracting consumers is always a challenging task for designers, which is why creatives should always express willingness and desire upon receiving any design brief. Without determination, creatives will not end up being successful in their quest for a creative solution, which should result in an influential solution at any cost. Having any sort of influence on consumers is seen as a successful achievement in the design industry. Any sort of affect consumers have on products means that the creative solution produced by designers was successful at producing a desired outcome. Such intentions are controlled by designers solely, since creative individuals set particular objectives prior to beginning a design process. Such aims and goals are discussed and are included in the objectives of an upcoming project. By accomplishing goals set from the beginning of a design process, creatives will have to wait and witness consumers' reactions in order to know if certain goals were achieved or not. So, by the time creative solutions are ready to sell, designers will be anxious to know if initial intentions would be successful or not.

Observing how consumers react to creative solutions will benefit designers greatly. Becoming aware of different reactions consumers may have towards products or solutions will help designers realise other ways in which to capture a consumer's attention. Studying how consumers react to elements of design will ease any production process facing designers. Demonstrating design principles whenever looking for creative solutions will be necessary for creatives, since the design process as a whole relies totally on certain principles that creatives should be aware of. Research, composition, typography, and colour are all considered design principles. Implementing creative skills while considering the principles of design will result in further imagination. In order to generate captivating ideas, creatives must be imaginative individuals who follow certain principles. Without understanding the fundamentals of design, creatives will be stuck and lost along an expected design process.

A situation of such will prevent creatives from achieving effective solutions. Simplicity is also another term creatives should have in mind whenever designing. Creative solutions which are simple in many ways could be even more impactful towards consumers. Sometimes creatives do not realise that the most simple yet straight forward idea may be the answer to multiple complicated cases. Surely developing simple ideas requires a complete understanding of negative space and alignment. By recognizing composition whenever designing, creatives will be able to produce well aligned and oriented results which will eventually please perceivers. Such results will lead the eyes to perceive information presented visually. Positioning design elements so that it pleases consumers' vision will be an effective method, because products will end up attracting consumers.

Layouts oriented in a specific way could also tempt perceivers instantly. Of course, scientific causes play a major role in such a case. Though creative individuals become the ones in charge of controlling such decisions. Authorizing creative decisions prior to production will leave creatives responsible for any costly decision, which will leave creatives totally accountable for any creative production. Therefore, creatives should always contemplate any design process seriously. Tasks of such importance will continue to be challenging for creatives, though by becoming aware of the actual target and understanding their reactions, creatives will be much more equipped. Preparing oneself for such a task requires confidence and mental strength from creatives. Designers will not be able to generate such effective ideas without desire, surely. Both consumers and perceivers depend on visual communication extensively. Producing creative solutions which continue to spread meaning through visual forms will always be essential. Creatives should protect an approach of such significance by developing influential solutions regularly. Always trying to attract and tempt consumers will attach perceivers even more to an approach like visual communication.

Throughout the years, visual communication has always been a successful matter. Perceivers of all kinds actually agree that communication transmitted visually is the most convenient way for many reasons. The perception of visual content is not only regarded as expressive, but totally influential as well. Conveying messages which are meaningful though entirely creative at the same time using visual forms encourages perceivers to react in an intended way. Such ways are different from one another since each and every creative solution developed has a desired target. Type design, for instance, is to do with developing typefaces for specific causes. Originally, typefaces are designed based on the purpose of the required need. By identifying where typefaces will be and what they will be used for, creatives will be able to produce a solution.

Without identifying a cause for an intended typeface, creatives would fail at achieving an effective response.

Typography basically expresses an existing language which is known to people. A language of such influence usually delivers meaning through visual forms from certain letters. Semantics is known as the field of linguistics and logic which deals which deals with meaning. Basically, the meaning of certain text and words is known as semantics. In the design industry, semantics is always considered a vital subject. Without understanding the importance of setting type so that it communicates, creatives would not be successful at having an impact on consumers or perceivers. Type design primarily will be the link between language and meaning in all cases facing designers. Therefore, by becoming aware of the significance regarding such a matter, creatives will be much more careful whenever developing or working with typefaces.

Typography should always be seen as a crucial principle in the design industry. Without typeface, visual communication would ultimately be incomplete. Type design is an example related to the influence visual communication has on both consumers and perceivers. Just like type design, advertising and branding also have such a marked influence on people. Branding for a sports event like the Olympics and the World Cup, for example, impact many perceivers of different categories. The target aimed at such an event does not only consist of athletes; coaches, fans, viewers, and journalists are all thought about prior to designing for such an event. Generally, during a major sporting event, perceivers are identified as anyone with an interest in sports. Whether they are actually around the proposed event or watching from home, anyone interested in an event of such will be noted as a perceiver.

Branding for such an event includes more than just a logo. Advertisement, signs, and symbols are also some of the major aspects included in a branding process. Guiding and directing fans and athletes to stadiums using visual communication will be part of a creative's intentions. Becoming aware of a specific surrounding through visual forms will result in an active system. In a case of such, the direction of perceivers relies totally on visual communication presented and displayed across the event's sites. So, by creating effective solutions which are meant to direct perceivers to a certain area, designers become successful at producing a desired result. An effect of such occurs only when creative solutions have an impact on an intended target. Whether creatives produce typefaces or design a branding project, anything developed should eventually be effective at some point.

Without being able to have an influence on perceivers or consumers, creatives would not be successful at conveying a visual message. Transmitting information through visually attractive solutions requires an intense understanding of such a subject. Creatives should never underestimate a project by any chance. Any design brief received should be seen as an opportunity, which is a decisive mission facing any designer. Having to consider a subject like visual communication with such admiration will lead creatives to become even more influential. Achieving an effective solution will always be challenging for creatives, though with respect and determination, creatives will be able to accomplish such tasks effectively.

Visual communication is an approach everyone relies on nowadays. Just thinking about the disappearance of such an approach will make everyone worry about functionality. Being able to perform personal tasks and needs while continuing to satisfy others based on their needs as well reveals characteristics of an effective system. Without the existence of visual communication, communities and societies would not be able to function. Basically, every living soul relies on visual communication in some way or another. Each individual perceives information regarding their own surrounding which is intentionally available to satisfy a desired target. Nearly each and every profession totally functions with some aspect of visual communication. Not only is visual communication at one's disposal, but obtainable at any period of time as well.

An approach of such is always accessible because everyone is actually surrounded by other features of the same field. A matter of such significance should always be recognised and valued by both perceivers and consumers. Without acknowledging a subject like visual communication, perceivers would not succeed at having aspirations. Something really interesting about visual communication is that over the years, the evolution of such a matter has not affected a certain area only, instead globally as well. A global affect is clearly noticed because visual forms of communication are being used in different parts of the world where it did not actually exist once. Every language known today somehow acquires a visual form of communication. Satisfying perceivers all over the world based on their own languages activates a system where communication becomes processed visually. Initiating a production process that depends on creativity will result in what is known as the design process. People are seen as the cause for communication to be visually transmitted. Commencing a design process based on certain requirements will lead to the development of creative solutions which tend to have a desired intention from creatives.

Both consumers and perceivers will continue to rely on

visual communication because of it being an accessible approach that never disappoints. As long as creatives understand consumers and perceivers, results would continue to have an influence on such individuals. Making sure that any result produced should be absolutely expressive while conveying a message will be necessary for creatives whenever developing designs. Without an impact that is evident on others creatives would basically fail at achieving an influential effect of any sort. Developing initial ideas to satisfy consumers will be crucial for creatives. Without maintaining satisfaction and approval of creative productions, designers would not be able to have an influence towards consumers.

By producing effective results, creatives become in charge of directing and guiding perceivers. Any perception of visual forms is certain to have an effect on perceivers. Some perceivers may not notice an effect at first, though when awareness strikes, perceivers will realise that a certain result had an impact on a decision or action, for instance. Visual communication has always been seen as an effective approach to communication. Without the presence of such an approach, the world would lack expressiveness. Communities would appear to be imperfect without visual communication. People would also be astray instead of directed. An impact of such is considered to be vital amongst creatives, perceivers, and consumers alike. The accessibility of visual communication makes it available for anyone at any time basically.

Distributed creative results is the reason for that approachability. Designers should always be individuals with great responsibility and accountability. Creatives who are able to succeed at attaining influential objectives. With such a mindset, creatives will be able to secure attention from perceivers much more easily, without complications. Attitude will always matter for creatives. No matter what mentality creatives have upon generating ideas, behaviour would greatly influence expected results.

A profession like design would always require willingness from creatives in order to be well prepared whenever facing any task. Since every individual depends on visual communication in many ways, design will always be an essential aspect. Being attached to visual forms of communication makes design essential for any user. Perceiving information visually has been the most convenient way of processing information. Therefore, consumers would always be perceiving creative solutions developed by creative individuals. As creatives, designers should be aware that developing any result requires careful study and understanding. Knowing more about the desired target will help creatives achieve pleasing results. Always having an influence towards perceivers will be the key to enabling visual communication. Having an intentional effect on perceivers will continue to enhance a matter like visual communication.

Creatives should be prepared whenever facing any task, because any result produced should be as effective as possible. By attracting perceivers with visually appealing results, creatives become successful at producing informative solutions. Such solutions should be clear to perceivers in order for a certain message to be conveyed. An approach like visual communication will continue to impact perceivers as long as creatives develop effective results. Transmitting messages and information through visual forms has evolved greatly over the years because of perceivers' reactions and responses. Learning from specific moments helps creatives improve the quality of creative solutions whenever processed. Generally, consumers' responses have benefited designers massively. By becoming aware of certain preferences, creatives become able to develop satisfying results all the time. Also, an approach like visual communication will continue to influence others as long as perception becomes enticing. Activating such an effect by producing creative results will benefit both perceivers and designers, since creatives will become credited for any achievement, while perceivers would gain consciousness. Spreading awareness through creative, visual forms will attach consumers even more, to visual communication. Always trying to please a desired target will be necessary and essential for creatives whenever producing creative solutions. By alluring consumers and perceivers, creatives will be in control of transmitting a visual message. Creative productions will always continue to be the link between information and meaning as long as creatives develop effective solutions.

# Chapter 14
## Executing Effective Design

Creative individuals are trained to produce results which satisfy others. In an industry like design especially, without accomplishing results which satisfy a desired target outcomes would not be successful. Effective design is an approach where creatives become in charge of producing creative solutions with an intended vision. Essentially, any creative solution that has an influence on perceivers which has been intended by creatives is known as an effective result. Without trying to achieve creative results, designers would not be able to capture perceivers' attention. Visual communication will always be seen as an effective approach of communication because of the instant effect on perceivers. Though, without creative individuals in charge of such a process, effective visual communication would not be successful at all. Therefore, creatives should always have in mind whenever designing that the purpose of design is to have an effect on others. Design can be effective in many ways; it all comes down to designers whenever coming up with effective solutions.

Everything creatives develop must have an intention at first. Without an intention, basically, creatives would not be able to achieve an effective outcome. Effective design will mainly rely on intentions from creatives, though the way in which creatives generate ideas will also affect any outcome yet to be produced. Designers should be aware of design principles prior to beginning any design process. Understanding how to deal with elements of design will greatly benefit creatives during a design process. In order for any creative solution to end being successful, an outcome must have some sort of influence on perceivers. A marked influence of such effect will reveal if a creative solution was effective or not. Producing visually communicative solutions requires a great amount of understanding and knowledge. By getting to know who the actual target is, creatives will be able to develop ideas based on certain needs from a specific target.

Having an overall idea of any actual target before designing will help creatives generate ideas more easily and precisely. Visual communication is not only considered to be effective towards perceivers only. Though visual communication is able to have an impact on any individual seeking information. What makes visual communication even more interesting is how creativity collides with logic to produce effective solutions, totally controlled by creative individuals who combine creative skills with thinking abilities in order to achieve such effective solutions. There is no doubt that visual communication depends entirely on creative individuals, without whom such an approach would not be successful at transmitting information. Creatives' presence is necessary for an industry like design, surely, though it is totally up to creatives to maintain such a level of vitality. Becoming active creatives by continuing to practice certain skills will eventually evolve individual abilities from creatives.

Developing individual characteristics will be crucial for creatives in the design industry, since outcomes would be greatly affected by experience. Gaining awareness from different experiences will result in informed individuals who understand the cause for designing. Executing effective design requires individuals who think creatively while generating ideas. By expressing creative skills and abilities right from the beginning, creatives will be able to achieve effective results continuously. Thought and desire will have a huge influence on designers. By being determined individuals, creatives will be able to achieve effective solutions more frequently without any complications. Producing effective results by designing in a creative yet innovative way is vital for creatives in the design industry. Effective creative solutions of such significance will always have a desired influence on others, without which visual communication would be unsuccessful and ineffective.

Designs produced and developed by creative individuals should have some sort of impact or influence on a specified target. Without an influence on a specified target, creatives would basically fail at transmitting a certain message. Designers are able to generate multiple ideas with such an affect. Though at times, most creatives would find some complications along the way. Before beginning any design process, creatives must be aware of the objectives behind a design brief. Understanding the cause to design will help creatives develop ideas based on certain needs. Which will eventually be effective towards an intended target. Visual communication as an approach which is substantial to many individuals will always be seen as an effective way of transmitting information. However, failure in achieving influential results will prevent the transmission of information visually. Also, perceivers would not be able to obtain meaning through visual forms of communication, which will directly result in an ineffective way of communication. Designs of any type should always end up being effective towards perceivers one way or another.

Without being successful at conveying a specific visual message, creatives would not have an effect on anyone. Whether creatives produce corporate or advertising solutions, outcomes should basically be intended in order to be effective towards a desired target. An intention from creatives will be crucial right from the start of a design process, since the purpose of having an intention is to guide creatives throughout a design process. By having an intention, creatives will be aware of who exactly the outcome would be intended for. Knowing the actual target will give creatives the opportunity to explore creative developments in order to best satisfy required needs. By doing so, creatives will instantly achieve responses from perceivers who have been targeted initially, which will result as being an effective approach towards perceivers. Achieving desired outcomes will reveal how successful creatives were at producing an effective solution.

Capturing a perceiver's attention requires more than understanding the target. Other aspects like appearance and elements are also considered vital subjects whenever designing. Paying attention to layouts and components will also be important for creatives to realise whenever designing, since appearance will be the first thing perceivers notice upon facing a creative production. Capturing attention from appearance will attract perceivers' attention while tempting individuals as well. An instant effect of such will be what creatives are always after whenever designing. Such an effect will continue to draw perceivers' attention while conveying a certain message. Designers should be aware that anything being developed should be effective one way or another. Effective design is achievable with development and exploration; without searching for a convenient solution, creatives would not be able to produce effective results. Any creative result produced and developed by creatives should result as effective towards a certain target. Not achieving results which are effective would greatly affect an approach like visual communication.

Since a visual form of communication will always rely on particular perceivers who are meant to obtain desired information in an appealing way. A way of such is managed totally by creative individuals, without who such an approach would certainly be ineffective by all means. Therefore, creative individuals should value a profession of such influence in order to realise the significance behind any result yet to be produced. Any creative production should be well thought about and carefully developed, since each and every outcome will most likely influence someone. Results with such impact are known as effective results because of designers' intentions to spread influence through visual forms. Creatives should always be aware of the purpose behind any design yet to be developed in order to achieve an effective solution. An industry like design will always be powerful in spreading influence through visual forms of communication. With passionate creatives at the helm, an industry of such significance will continue to evolve to the best.

Achieving effective design depends on certain principles controlled entirely by creatives. Apart from having an intention prior to designing, creatives should also consider visual balance in order to achieve effective designs. Visual balance is regarded as balanced outcomes where elements in a specific design are very well distributed to capture attention. Considering visual balance while designing will result in well-uniformed layouts which ease the conveyance process towards perceivers.

Creatives should understand that in order for a creative solution to be effective, capturing attention will be the key to attract perceivers. Attention becomes hard to attract only if certain outcomes do not meet perceivers needs. In this case, anything produced becomes totally ineffective towards perceivers. As creatives, designers would not want to experience such moments because of failing to achieve successful outcomes at times, though such experiences may occur.

However, it will totally be up to creatives to figure a way and bounce back, since failing to do so will result in even more disaster which would not be acceptable. Learning to deal with unexpected situations will always benefit creatives, though creatives at this point should be aware of the cause of such failure in order to recover and enhance individual abilities. Becoming aware of slight details related to capturing attention will help creatives develop even better creative solutions, which will result as effective towards a certain group of perceivers. Exploring certain layouts, for example, will allow creatives to test perceivers based on appearance. Also studying ways in which perceivers become attached to creative solutions will help creatives generate guaranteed ideas. Negative space and visual hierarchy are vital whenever considering visual balance.

Becoming able to experiment with adjustments and grids will give creatives a better understanding of different ways to attract perceivers. Alignment in design is regarded as a crucial principle. Arranging elements in a specific way to appear uniformed and structured will have a great effect on perceivers. Creatives may experiment with multiple techniques and styles at this stage in a design process. Anything creatives eventually produce should express creativity while conveying a visual message. Layouts and appearance lie under creativity from this aspect, though other elements like typography and colour are also seen as the creative aspect of design. Each and every element creatives decide to implement in a creative solution will have a part in conveying a visual message. The importance of such elements will be as important as the actual message itself. Without creative elements, solutions will not be accomplished in a successful way. Basically, the implementation of such creative elements will define a creative solution. Therefore, paying attention to how perceivers react to certain elements will give creatives an advantage whenever coming up with further creative solutions.

Once creatives complete an intended yet creative solution, results will soon be effective towards a specified target. The process of achieving effective design requires a total understanding of the fundamentals of design before beginning any design process. By realizing the importance of each and every element, a design might consist of, creatives will be prepared to face any expected task. Raising awareness levels will benefit individual knowledge, which will greatly affect thinking abilities in creatives. Knowledgeable creatives will be wiser whenever generating ideas that will greatly influence a creative's intention. Any effect on a creative's intention will somehow affect the outcome. So, by having positive characteristics, creatives will be able to achieve effective solutions by designing in an innovative way. Confident designers will always generate effective ideas frequently without any difficulties. Creatives should always seek information that is productive yet informative, especially regarding perceivers, since the more creatives study perceivers, the easier it will be to develop effective solutions which best suit certain needs.

Another vital aspect of achieving effective design is creativity; the one and only attribute creatives could not function without. Imaginative and original ideas initiate creativity from designers. Without the ability to think in such an imaginative way, creatives would not be able to develop creative solutions which are supposed to be effective. Creativity towards designers will always be essential, since creative outcomes depend solely on designers' thoughts and ideas. Being able to generate such influential ideas may, at times, take a twist. Surely there will be moments where creatives become unable to generate such ideas as a result of lack of inspiration. Sources of inspirations may sometimes be unavailable or unattainable since creatives become in complete control of the search for inspirations. Such moments may lead creatives to unanticipated sources of inspirations, which could be even more influencing towards creatives.

Searching for an inspiration prior to designing is crucial for designers, not just because of a certain influence an inspiration might have on an outcome, but also because inspirations are known to be the reason behind creativity. Being inspired by surroundings, for instance, may cause feelings to have an influential affect, which will eventually affect any decisions creatives intend to make. Any sort of object, moment, or even a thought may be inspiring towards creatives. It is without the occurrence of such causes that will prevent creatives from inspirations. Also, inspiring moments or objects will greatly influence the way designers react to decision making, which in an industry like design is very crucial. During a design process, creatives develop many phases of the actual final outcome. So, by being influenced by anything, basically, creatives will also be affected whenever making decisions.

For creatives, being influenced by anything that triggers creativity will be vital towards any outcome. Since creatives produce and create results that should express meaning while also being innovative at the same time. Creativity requires skill and influence in order to generate. Without a certain knowledge about principles and fundamentals, creatives will not be able to accomplish any creative task. Influence as well is necessary for creatives, which without creatives would not have the urgency to think creatively. As an attribute, creativity will be essential for creatives during a design process. Lack of creativity and innovation will affect creative outcomes greatly. Since effective results become affected by how creatives control a design process. Preventing an inspiration from occurring will have a great impact on a designer's performance. Therefore, as creative individuals, designers should always search for an inspirational source in order to commence creative thinking. Developing effective design relies on many factors creatives disregard at times due to inessential thoughts. However, realizing the importance of such factors like creativity may increase chances of success yet to be achieved.

Effective design will be achievable for creatives who are well aware of the essentials, such as creatives who demonstrate skill and knowledge to seek creativity. Performance will always be affected in personal ways, though it is up to creatives for such ways to have an instant effect on creativity. Once creatives feel the desire to create, ideas will soon be implemented, and solutions will begin to shape up. Developing ideas from initial inspirations and influences will raise the level of quality from creative outcomes designers intend to produce. Levels of creativity from an outcome will greatly be influenced by inspirations as well. Any creative thought designers obtain over time will be the cause of an inspiration. Being exposed to different surroundings will increase the chances of inspirations, surely. Therefore, heading to different places or visiting new locations will help creatives be aware of interesting facts and information, which will certainly have an affect towards any outcome.

Raising awareness levels will continue to affect the creativity a designer obtains. Following unexpected paths will raise awareness of compelling subjects. As creatives, designers should always be prepared to explore informative locations in search for an inspiration. By securing inspiring influences, creatives will be full of imaginative ideas that need to be executed. Accomplishing creative solutions with imaginative ideas will greatly influence perceivers which results as effective. An effective approach then becomes easily achieved if results continue to be as influential as they should be. Without an effect on perceivers through creative solutions, a successful impact would not be achieved. Effective results will be the key to capturing attention in order to have an influence, which without creativity, such an approach would not be successful or influential at all.

While implementing creative skills, designers express creative abilities by exploring various elements. Creativity then becomes gradually revealed upon completing a creative outcome. Every outcome creatives produce must have an impact on perceivers in order to be effective. Creative solutions have the power to influence perceivers instantly as long as such solutions result as appealing. Trying to capture a perceiver's attention is always seen as a challenging task. However, creatives will be able to achieve effective results because of creative abilities each designer obtains. Designers are skilled individuals who express imaginative thinking abilities in an efficient way. Therefore, searching for a convenient resolution will be possible by demonstrating certain skills. Producing effective results surely depends on mastering the basics. Creatives should express knowledge and understanding whenever designing in order to be successful. For creatives, a design process is where experimenting occurs. So, developing creative ideas at such a stage of exploration will greatly affect any outcome yet to be achieved. Creatives should be aware that creative solutions produced should transmit a visual message to perceivers in order to result as effective.

Visual communication is an approach regarding the transmission of communication visually. As creatives, designers become responsible for developing such results by implementing creative elements to form an outcome. Designers basically develop creative ideas based on perceivers needs in order to accomplish an effective result. Transmitting communication visually calls for precise concentration whenever designing and developing solutions. Anything creatives develop will be visually perceived. Therefore, appearance will always be vital, surely. Considering the layouts of certain elements will be crucial for creatives whenever designing. Achieving creative results with appealing features will tempt perceivers frequently. Like all other creative elements, typography is a critical element for creatives. Typography is the field of letterforms and typefaces where art collides with science to form appealing results. Also, typography is regarded as one of the main design principles for creatives. Such a vital subject makes visual communication possible because of the distribution of letterforms which expresses a certain language. Arrangement of typefaces may seem like a simple task, though most designers struggle to set type in an effective way.

Typefaces can be artistic, straight forward, or condensed, since different styles of typefaces have been constantly developed. Also, typefaces are classified into certain type families based on how each type appears. A field like typography makes visual communication even more effective, since arranged type may convey information to perceivers who are aware of the same language being portrayed. Letterforms eventually are meant for language purposes. For creatives, having the authority to develop typefaces in order to satisfy perceivers makes it even more challenging. Making sure that typefaces developed are comprehended by perceivers will cause any creative result to end up being effective. Creative results depend on multiple elements designers generate; especially typography as an element will be crucial to producing effective design. Including type elements into any creative result adds form and structure to a complete design. The appearance of type also compels perceivers to react in a specific way. Typography should not be seen as just a way to express a particular language; instead, typography will continue to be an essential element to spread communication. An indispensable element like typography will continue to influence perceivers who seek any sort of communication.

Creatives handling typography should be extremely careful whenever developing creative outcomes, since the appearance of type will greatly affect perceivers. Therefore, arranging type in a convenient way that somehow appears to be appealing will be crucial for designers looking to achieve effective results. Designers generally develop creative ideas to influence perceivers in many ways. Such an intention from creatives will directly affect any outcome creatives tend to produce. By preparing oneself to achieve such influential results, creatives will be able to develop effective designs more frequently.

Creative skills and elements will be primary features of any effective result creatives eventually develop. Without which such influence and impact would not be achievable at all. Implementing certain elements with creative thinking skills will be supportive for designers looking to have an impact towards perceivers. With such an understanding of the creative industry, designers will continue to develop effective solutions which are influential.

Once creatives succeed at implementing such creative skills, individual abilities will begin to improve gradually. With constant practice, designers immediately develop confidence whenever designing. For creatives especially, confidence will be important whenever developing creative ideas. Having any sort of belief in achieving effective designs will help creatives be more confident during a design process. Also, what is really important about having confidence is the success that is yet to follow. Since whatever creatives actually create will eventually be intended for a certain group of perceivers. By being creatives who are constantly active, designers also gain further experience, which is very vital for creative individuals who attempt to achieve effective results. Experiences creatives encounter shape up individual characteristics from designers. Going through certain experiences raises awareness levels from creative individuals. Creatives who are always active in practice have a better chance at developing successful results compared with inexperienced creatives. Lack of knowledge and experience towards an industry like design makes it difficult for creatives during any developments process. Being creatives who are well informed and experienced will greatly influence creatives to perform at a professional level.

For creatives, experience will always be beneficial, no matter what the moment might be. Creatives may gain experience even from self-commissioned jobs, which are meant to obtain creativity so that it remains at a constant level, since some creatives may at times be unemployed, especially if creatives are freelancing. However, for creatives who are employed, experience may be the everyday encounters designers may go through or face. Whatever beneficial moments creatives may experience will greatly affect personal characteristics that designers maintain. In an industry like design, experienced creatives will easily be noticed amongst others. Performance and knowledge a creative attains will reveal experience levels creatives already have gained. Therefore, constantly being active by surrounding oneself with knowledgeable creatives will improve individual characteristics from a designer. Gradually developing experience will result in professional creatives who are aware of what a profession like design demands. Also, by developing an individual understanding, creatives become aware of the importance of developing effective design.

Beginning to gain experience from certain moments will help creatives establish a solid foundation whenever designing, since experienced creatives become professional individuals who have a concern towards any outcome. Such a concern will direct creatives to producing effective design which directly influences perceivers. Normally individuals who are regarded as professionals are individuals who are able to deal with such demanding work. Abilities each individual maintains are always able to improve over time. With experiences, for instance, such abilities gradually develop and become part of an individual. For designers specifically, gaining knowledge from certain experiences will always be beneficial. It is up to creatives of course to gain experience, though by expressing creative skills in an efficient way, designers will be able to attract attention instantly. Creatives with experience will always have sufficient abilities to perform in an effective way. Originally, it is with experience that designers actually become aware of an intended group of perceivers. Also, finding a solution which best satisfies certain perceivers will be achievable way easier with experience in hand, keeping in mind that by gaining experience, designers will develop an understanding of a situation either a present one or one yet to come.

Without developing knowledge, creatives would not be able to achieve effective solutions which best satisfy an intended group of people. Becoming aware of the target eases any development process, however with experience of a certain situation, creatives become much more confident in solving any problem yet to be faced. Basically, greater experience of any subject will always enhance individual abilities. Creatives should realise that strengthening individual abilities with greater experience will be advantageous towards a final outcome. Knowledgeable creatives will be more likely to succeed at achieving effective results frequently because of the amount of experience gained. By gaining knowledge from certain experiences, creatives will evolve into proficient individuals who are aware of effective ways which are successful towards perceivers.

Trying to execute effective design requires awareness and creativity from designers. Creatives are certainly able to achieve certain skills with constant practice. Developing understanding constantly will help creatives achieve effective results whenever designing. Becoming aware that the reason to produce effective results is to maintain an approach like visual communication will be vital. Designers are regarded as creative individuals who have the ability to influence perceivers. In order to create such influential results, creatives must implement certain skills. By considering the elements of design prior to designing, creatives will be able to achieve successful results. Also, having the intention to produce such effective results will be crucial towards any outcome yet to be achieved.

Overall, as creatives, designers should be creative individuals who excel at implementing fundamental skills in order to achieve an influential response towards perceivers. Effective design is about producing design that is successful at having a desired affect towards an intended target. Creatives must design for a cause in order to achieve an effective response. Visual communication is always considered the approach which spreads communication in the most effective way. Continuing to have such an effect from perceivers requires creative solutions which are impactful by every sense. Once certain aspects are completed in an effective way, creative solutions are completed and presented visually to attract perceivers. Having a successful response from perceivers indicates that any creative solution developed is regarded as an effective solution. Without a successful outcome, creatives would have developed an ineffective solution, which typically fails at having a marked influence on perceivers. Therefore, having any sort of influence on perceivers with creative results is necessary for an effective visual communication approach. Without effective designs, visual communication would not be successful at delivering certain messages.

Creatives should realise that an approach like visual communication depends entirely on creative results which should be effective. It is up to creatives to achieve such results by implementing creative skills and understanding. Without the development of effective designs, visual communication will eventually be incomplete by lacking a successful response. Everything creatives intend on producing should one way or another result as effective towards a certain group of perceivers. Visual communication as an approach is meant to have an influence on both consumers and perceivers by the development of creative solutions which constantly have to be effective. Designers should always have the desire to develop creative solutions with an impact towards others. Only with such an influence will creatives be successful at achieving effective results. Creativity and knowledge will continue to guide creatives throughout a design process, though by being determined, creatives will continue to develop influential solutions for perceivers.

# Chapter 15
## Creativity from a Global Perspective

Everyone agrees that creativity has and will always be the force behind craftsmanship of any sort. Creativity basically drives creatives to express imaginative ideas while implementing certain skills. Any creation developed by creatives will eventually result as appealing. Of course, such results require particular skills and understanding, though as creatives, craftsmen as well were once seen as individuals with creative abilities. Nowadays, craftsmen are also known as artisans or designers, however back in the day craftsmen dealt with much tougher work, which was mainly handmade. Craftsmanship from the past is widely appreciated today because of the skill and effort displayed to achieve such results. Whether craftsmen are skilled with certain objects or trained to use certain programmes like designers, creativity would still be the major factor behind any production yet to be developed. Creativity is the reason behind compelling productions and solutions developed by talented individuals. Certain cultures today still recognise creative creations as part of tradition.

Creativity will continue to flourish as long as creatives express imaginative thinking abilities. Also, certain creative productions will keep influencing others to create in an artistic way. Inspirations may be influential at any time or place, so the existence of creative works globally may actually inspire any individual at any time. Creative individuals are known to generate creative ideas from different surroundings. Therefore, becoming aware of other creative productions globally will continue to force creatives whenever developing ideas. For designers especially, creativity should be seen as an influential matter.

Depending on how each creative reacts to creative works, inspirations may strike suddenly and will totally be affected by a specific moment. As long as creatives become aware of the value behind a certain production or solution, appreciation will soon follow to initiate a creative thought. A basic thought will then develop into an idea which basically evolves into a final outcome. A creative process of such intricacy requires exploring individuals who are always in search of creativity from different sources. Surely becoming a creative explorer requires a great amount of effort, though every single minute from a journey of such would raise awareness levels from creatives. Raising awareness will also have an effect on the development of certain skills creatives may obtain, since creatives gain knowledge while exploring, which will also raise experience levels each individual secures. By gradually developing knowledge, creatives become more experienced towards a creative profession. Especially in an industry like design, experience will always be vital, since creatives with experience become dependable and reliable whenever controlling any design process.

Surely the knowledge gained from certain experiences affects creatives to perform in a professional level. Though it will always be an impact which creatives have gained that is actually forcing creatives to perform at such a level. Expanding knowledge and understanding by exploring creative works form centuries ago or even current developments will greatly influence creatives even more. Witnessing what other craftsman have achieved gives creatives even more desire to create and become inventive. For such a creative industry to thrive, creatives must be professional individuals who appear to be experienced from the creative past. Executing effective solutions in a creative way will always require creatives who are aware of what a profession like design demands. Creativity is the reason behind every creative solution developed by designers, without which solutions would lack effectiveness, by all means. Whether creatives create to impress clients or their own self, what actually matters most is the degree of creativity each designer attains or possesses over time. Creativity will continue to be the source behind design and craftsmanship as long as creative individuals become inventive while developing productions, which will greatly help the creative industry to thrive.

Basically, the term creativity translates to the implementation of imaginative ideas in order to produce compelling yet innovative results. Designers as creative individuals are meant to produce such results constantly. Creativity inspires creatives to create and become inventive, surely, though creativity will always require a certain amount of effort to be maintained. Creative individuals seek inspirations from many surroundings best suitable for each individual. Any attempt creatives might consider will eventually have an influence on creatives. Since creativity does not occur all of a sudden, it will be up to creatives to try and attain such force. Design fundamentals and principles also affect creativity, though inspirations become the vital source, since inspirations enable any creative process to function smoothly. Inspirations may be anything creatives regard as a source that causes designers to generate creative thoughts. Without seeking inspirations, creatives would fail at achieving successful results. Therefore, as designers, creative individuals should always be aware of multiple subjects that may be inspirational at any time.

Subjects may include anything designers see as interesting to be explored. Whether creatives prefer to explore historic sites, museums, or monuments: anything creatives wish to explore will one way or another inspire creatives to become imaginative. Globally, there are many known destinations which offer such inspiring developments. Creatives may consider any development as part of an inspiration. Since certain developments were once developed for a specific cause. Looking into interesting subjects will help creatives realise that the importance of creating lies beyond satisfaction. Fulfilling one's wish may sound appropriate, though leaving an imprint while developing a creative idea will certainly be even more rewarding. Designers are creatives, just like craftsmen whose productions are meant to be innovative yet appealing towards others. Apart from having creative characteristics, such developments should also be influential. Any creation or outcome that continues to influence people will always be appreciated. Once creatives reach or get to a certain amount of appreciation, acknowledgement would soon follow.

Recognizing any creative development with such value and respect does not only state success towards creatives, though such a reaction would also cause an influence by having a continuous impact towards perceivers. Spreading influence through creative productions would continue to influence creatives from different generations which future creatives would also be part of. Craftsmen and designers are similar in many ways because of the creative purposes both individuals maintain. Craftsmen of today may still be identified as creatives just like designers, since objectives from both parties are related to the creative industry. Each creative individual may develop imaginative ideas their own ways, though any outcome would still be regarded as a creative result from both designers and craftsmen. Often creatives would find inspirations from other creative creations much more effective than sources that lack creativity. From a creative perspective, that sort of reaction would be totally acceptable, since creatives always love to compete with one another which eventually results in a positive way, initially such possible challenges in an industry like design would give creatives an opportunity to become even more imaginative.

Inspirations from creative developments would always be exciting to explore, and somehow develop thinking abilities from creatives. Inquiring and investigating about a certain creative development will raise awareness from creatives while influencing individuals to be as creative as possible. Accessible creative works are available everywhere, however designers will always require an effort to reach such sites. Without willingness, designers would not be able to achieve such effective results. So, as creatives, having the desire to explore creative diversity will greatly influence designers upon generating ideas and developing creative thoughts. Inspirations will begin to flow, and creatives become full of imaginative ideas waiting to be implemented. Creativity will always be seen as a source, where inspirations begin to unfold so that innovative ideas are developed. Designers should always be creatives who are aware of multiple creative surroundings and sites. With knowledge of the creative arts and its offerings, designers become acquainted with useful facts and information regarding the creative world, which will greatly affect creative individuals personally and professionally. Surely, experiences gained from any quest will transform thinking abilities designers obtain over time. As a result, knowledgeable creatives will continue to develop professional skills an industry like design demands for.

Creative individuals will always need inspirations to begin developing ideas of any sort. Without such influencing sources, creatives would not be able to function as designers. Creativity depends on how designers react whenever developing an outcome. Anything developed by designers would have an inspiration which aided the design process in actually being completed. Without a creative source, designers would feel lost and somehow imperfect. Generally, creativity would be judged upon the completion of an outcome. Therefore, designers would require to back up any solution with an actual inspiration. An initial source of inspiration would be the cause to creative productions and solutions designers are likely to develop. By exploring creative sites around the world, designers basically expand awareness levels. Each designer would have personal ways which are personally suitable to approach such sites.

Since some creatives prefer to approach certain places in the most convenient way, which is the best possible, creative works around the globe are recognised based on fame and popularity, mostly, though some creative creations remain forgotten about and unnoticed. It is up to creatives to research such dismissed creative sources in order to get a chance and explore inspiring works. Many cultures around the world have artistic influences as part of tradition, for instance. Morocco is regarded as one of those countries where creative works are widely recognised as part of its culture. Especially for visiting creatives from other parts of the world, Morocco would always be an inspiring country to explore. From the historic architecture to the creative crafts and zellige artwork, Morocco is surely filled with creativity in every corner one decides to explore. Something special about Morocco is that every city has something exceptional to offer, especially for creative individuals. Marrakesh, for example, is a city located in the southern part of Morocco. Known for its architectural influences and vibrant colours. Jardin Majorelle is one of the major places visitors of Morocco explore. The garden is divided into two parts, which is the botanical garden and the artist's landscape garden. Many tourists enjoy walks around Jacques Majorelle's original garden.

Surely the landscaping and architecture are so inspiring because of the combination of French and Moroccan influences portrayed. Anyone wandering through such lush surroundings would feel refreshed instantly. Also located in Marrakesh is the Bahia Palace, which was built in the late nineteenth century, mainly another tourist attraction because of the Islamic architecture displayed across the landmark. Bahia in Arabic refers to brilliance, which reveals the initial intention of such a development. The palace is widely known for the detailed zellige artwork displayed on the walls all over the entire palace. Zellige artwork requires ultimate skill in order to be accomplished. Basically, 'zellige' is how Moroccans refer to tile work. Anyone who is aware of such an art would understand Islamic patterns and geometry, which is beautifully displayed in nearly each and every single Moroccan inspired architecture. Another famously recognised site in Marrakesh is Koutoubia, which is considered the largest mosque in Marrakesh. Originally, Koutoubia was founded in 1147, known for its captivating architecture and prominent minaret which is considered as a major landmark around Morocco. Also, Koutoubia expresses Islamic architecture in the most original way possible.

For creatives specifically, exploring a site like Koutoubia would certainly be a mesmerizing and unmissable opportunity. Since artistic values from historic times are revealed, which shows creative capabilities at a time when such achievements were difficult to accomplish. Just like Marrakesh, other cities like Casablanca, Fes, Tangier, and Chefchaouen are all worth exploring. From the blue jewel located in the Rif Mountains to the striking architecture across the Mediterranean and Atlantic Seas, Morocco is certainly a country bursting with alluring yet original creativity.

Being original to one's own roots and developing creative works based on traditional values gives any production remarkable significance. Morocco will always be noticed as a source which truly expresses Islamic art and architecture because of the way tradition is respected and valued, which continues to influence generations of craftsmen yet to come. Islamic art will always evoke creatives' interest because of the intricate details displayed to achieve creative results. Also, Islamic art is widely recognised upon three continents (Africa, Asia, and Europe) which shows how diverse a particular art can be. Creativity is surely an influential term which continues to captivate people all over the world. A specific art with Islamic influences is surely known to be an intense subject because of creative varieties such an art displays. Creative individuals would agree that an art like Islamic art would always be interesting to explore. Enthralling developments makes such an art so fascinating, especially towards creatives.

Known by many as one of the most creative arts ever developed since centuries ago, Islamic art represents traditions and cultures from all over the world, which reveals how an art of such has influences around three different continents. Islamic art continues to inspire individuals globally because of the various art forms such an art consists of. Geometric patterns, calligraphy, tile work, and architecture are all considered to be as aspects of Islamic art. Something extremely unique and special about Islamic art is that developments from such influences are accessible across Europe, Asia, and Africa. Islamic influences which expand across three continents explains the creative diversity within one particular art. Surely Islamic art is recognised as a rich and lavish subject amongst creatives. That is because of the detailed and intricate productions accomplished from centuries ago and still ongoing.

Such credit will have to be awarded to all the craftsmen and creatives who have greatly collaborated to achieve such creative outcomes which to this day continues to inspire creatives from all over the world. Appreciating such developments because they exist reveals how difficult it was to actually achieve such a creative development of any sort. Most creatives today find that exploring art from centuries ago becomes much more inspiring than art developed recently. Surely the effort and endeavour displayed at a time when certain tools and equipment were difficult to obtain, in order to achieve such captivating productions makes anyone appreciate the creative outcome in a special way, since craftsmanship back in the day was seen as a profession that required a vigorous amount of effort. Compared to creatives nowadays, even if creative works today required that amount of effort to achieve compelling outcomes, there will always be an alternative way available for creatives.

Software programmes nowadays make productions much easier to develop compared to decades or even centuries ago. Therefore, creatives will always appreciate historic creative works which have been developed the original way without recent technology. Calligraphy works from the Ottoman Empire in Turkey, for instance, expresses extreme accuracy from every aspect. Precision in such creative works were all achieved by hand, since the art of calligraphy is attained by ink and water with the force of skilled creatives. Calligraphy works can be seen all over Turkey, especially around Istanbul which once was the capital city of the Ottomans. Turkish calligraphy is known to be artistic and neat. Quranic verses or Arabic phrases are displayed with ultimate accuracy to convey messages the Islamic way. Calligraphy works with Turkish influences can be seen around the Topkapi Palace Museum which once was the residence of all the Ottoman Sultans. Also, the Topkapi Museum displays many works of art which dates back to the fifteenth and sixteenth century during the Ottoman Empire, works that express creativity in many ways which has been achieved centuries ago. Tile work with Islamic influences, patterns and motifs around each and every corner, and the overall architecture of the palace just sums up creativity in one word.

Anyone experiencing such artistry would instantly feel captivated, not just because of the craftsmanship displayed, though the effort in achieving such an influential development makes anyone appreciate creative capabilities. Just like Turkey, India as well is regarded as one of the chief destinations which represents Islamic art. Mughal India was founded during the early sixteenth century, which saw vast developments and major monuments become part of the country's whole culture. Ever since the Mughals conquered India, creative works began to evolve and emerge across many cities. Mughal art includes wonderful creative motifs inspired from nature, tile work, and prominent architecture known to be like no other. Mughals basically refers to the people of the Mughal Empire which includes rulers, soldiers, craftsmen, and anyone belonging to the Empire.

Originally, the Mughal Empire lasted for over three hundred years, which enforced many notable developments that continue to inspire and attract people globally. Such developments include the Taj Mahal in Agra, and the Red Fort in New Delhi. Many other developments with Mughal influences were commissioned by multiple Mughal emperors during the active years of the Mughal Empire, which actually expanded from east to west of India and part of Pakistan today around the seventeenth century. Mughal motifs are known for being inventive yet original because of influences from natural surroundings. Floral Mughal motifs are seen in nearly every Mughal development left to be witnessed. Whether such creative arts are displayed on walls or tiles, an identity can still be noticed upon gazing at such creative works. Also, to this day Mughal motifs have been influencing creatives to implement such styles on fabrics, products, and creative works. Block printing, for instance, is recognised as a creative art where carved wood blocks are compressed on fabrics or other surfaces to reveal certain patterns and designs. Such an active art to this day in India still uses Mughal motifs to design with, which continues to inspire anyone because of a creative affect.

Today, Mughal influences are recognised not just around India but worldwide, as well. Creativity will always be behind such an influence, though developing a creative identity which becomes known and appreciated by many reveals triumph one has achieved, which the Mughals as well have certainly accomplished over time. Surely creativity will continue to inspire creatives from many various backgrounds. Appreciating and acknowledging the fact that other Empires from centuries ago, for example, have achieved such compelling developments and works of art makes any creative individual realise that the purpose of creating is more about expressing an identity than achieving fame. Revealing one's own roots by implementing traditional values whenever being creative causes outcomes to become more worthy and notable. Creative individuals should have confident characters who approve of taking risks in order to achieve effective outcomes. Creatives from the past centuries who have achieved such notable developments which continue to inspire creatives of today have been set as the perfect example because of the tremendous effort displayed to achieve such influential results. Creatives today should realise the importance behind such creative developments in order to keep developing influential results constantly.

Most creatives do not realise that creativity naturally intensifies thinking. At times, creative individuals become so overwhelmed from certain surroundings, and somehow dismiss the affects which might occur later. Thinking abilities gradually develop from experiences anyone might face. Creatives as well become affected from certain surroundings without even being noticed. Experiences creatives may encounter at any time or place will always have an influence on creatives one way or another. Therefore, exploring creative works from around the world will always be a positive matter which greatly affects creatives. Expanding one's awareness and knowledge always requires effort and desire. Creatives with a passionate character will always have an advantage upon generating ideas during any design process. Enhancing knowledge will further allow creatives to develop influential thinking skills more frequently. By exploring creative works and developments, individuals gradually develop a deeper understanding of subjects. For creatives especially, such an affect would greatly impact any outcome yet to be developed. Designers as creative individuals always need an active way of thinking in order to develop creative solutions. Without constant activity, creatives basically become ineffective because of a deficient level of creativity.

Lack of creativity instantly effects any design process, since imaginative thinking becomes prevented, which clearly explains the significance of creativity, not just as a source but an influential matter as well. Creativity from any effective source will be influential towards creatives in many ways, not just towards inspirations, but thinking abilities would progress and develop as well. Enhanced thinking develops gradually based on certain experiences designers may encounter at any time. Therefore, as creatives, designers should always expand knowledge and awareness in order to achieve effective solutions. There would not be a better way to expand understanding than to explore various cultures and developments of the past. History will always be a useful asset for creatives. Not just because of valuable resources which are accessible anywhere, but also because of the obtainable references any history may offer. Anyone in search of creativity may be directed to historic sites and places which are notable and remarkable for many aspects. Creatives who experience and explore such sites will gradually develop an understanding of certain subjects, places, or people who were once part of such developments. Creatives would then be aware of interesting facts and information which will clearly affect the way in which creatives think to generate creative yet imaginative ideas.

Thinking creatively will require a vigorous amount of effort before beginning to generate thoughts. Creatives should have the desire to explore in order to gain awareness of stimulating subjects, which may greatly affect thinking abilities that develop creative solutions which are meant to be effective in many ways. Creativity from creative works will intensify a designer's thinking by affecting the way in which a designer processes an idea of any sort. Realizing the effort behind a certain production will make creatives want to accomplish effective outcomes that influence people. Designers may observe creative works from the past or present in search for an inspiration that might strike to aid a design process, though thinking becomes effected first prior to an inspiration being activated. Creative minds are able to generate ideas much faster, though backing up an individual's memory with useful information will act like a resourceful way upon generating ideas. Creatives should consider such an approach in order to think in an imaginative yet original way whenever developing creative thoughts.

Designers are regarded as individuals with vast creative abilities. As creatives, designers become easily influenced from certain surroundings. Creative works which have been developed by fellow creatives will always act like a source of inspiration for any creative individual. Appreciating such creative developments gives designers an opportunity to produce even more inventive works. Surely influences from around the world may inspire creatives to think in an imaginative way. Since creativity requires effort and constant practice in order to be maintained. Designers should realise that the more informative a creative happens to be, the better chance of being influential creatives will eventually be. Influential results will continue to act as a source of inspiration while having an impact towards others. Creative works or developments may certainly have an influence on anyone as much as creatives. The production of any creative outcome would be as inspirational towards creatives as any other individual from various professions.

Creative works, developments, and solutions are all produced with the intention of having an impact towards a desired target. Literally all creatives should also be aware of such an intention prior to designing, since the purpose of developing compelling creative solutions is spreading influence while effecting others. Having such a desired impact on others reveals whether creative solutions end up being effective or not towards people. Eventually, ineffective solutions or outcomes would never be recognised or appreciated as much since the initial purpose was not achieved. An industry like the creative industry will always aim to spread some sort of influence and somehow impact other individuals. It is how craftsmen from centuries ago and creatives of today have been functioning, with the exact same intention in mind. Designers as creative individuals will always be tempted to explore other creative works in search of inspiration. Learning from creative productions and studying the process behind such achievements will greatly benefit designers. Inquisitive creatives will be more likely to succeed because of the amount of information a creative obtains from certain experiences.

Designers who gain knowledge from inspiring surroundings will eventually develop imaginative thinking abilities more frequently. Creatives with an informed state of mind will act and perform like knowledgeable professionals. For creatives especially, information and understanding matters greatly because outcomes become instantly effected. Which is why being influenced by creative works is one way to secure an inspiration that activates creative thoughts. However, researching in depth about certain developments will reveal much more interesting facts and information that are extremely influential in many ways. Inventiveness requires complete awareness; creatives, however, will always be after creativity to attempt such imaginative solutions. Though extensive awareness about certain subjects will reveal fascinating information which will arouse curiosity from designers.

As creatives, designers should follow an inventive path and search for useful resources that might enable creative thinking designers possess. Numerous attempts and experiences would improve thinking abilities massively. Which will greatly affect an individual who processes ideas frequently. Creativity will continue to inspire creatives as long as creatives search for interesting facts. Influences may affect anyone at any time or place. Such an effect on creatives would be extremely vital towards the production of an effective outcome. Also, a marked influence on creatives would greatly affect the generation of creative ideas, which should be imaginative in order to be successful. Creativity will be an accessible source for anyone with the desire to impact others.

Craftsmen and creatives are both seen as imaginative individuals who continue to influence others. Creativity causes such skills to thrive and constantly develop. As creative individuals, designers should understand that creative solutions should result as effective in order to have an impact on a desired target. Creativity as a source will continue to inspire creatives of today and creatives yet to come. Developments around the globe with creative aspects will continue to evoke anyone's interest, especially for creatives. Researching creative developments known globally and learning about the history behind such works will benefit creatives greatly. Inspirations are available anywhere, basically; it is up to creatives to display an effort and begin searching for such inspiring sources. With constant practice, creatives will be able to generate innovative ideas which are backed with creative sources. Creative skills as well are also developed with an in depth understanding of certain subjects. Designers should expand individual awareness by constantly researching about interesting works of art which have a great history behind them.

Learning from the masters of the past will make creatives wiser, surely, compared to creatives who lack awareness. Creative developments are known to spread influence while having an impact on other individuals. Globally recognised creative developments have been inspiring many generations in many possible ways. Any sort of influence on an individual is caused because of an initial intention. Creativity has the power to affect anyone without even realizing, though if ceased, everyone would notice its significance right away. The existence of creative works helps reveal certain identities and cultures that have been ignored and disregarded for quite a while. Recognizing such developments and acknowledging the way in which they have been structured will certainly make anyone appreciate the effort displayed to achieve such interesting results. Designers who explore various cultures and creative works will be regarded as experienced creatives. Creatives who are aware of vital yet useful information which supports any creative process and broadens understanding possessed. Awareness will surely cause inspirations to flow regularly, therefore creatives should be eager to explore multiple creative works which are influential in many ways. Creativity from around the globe will continue to be a source of inspiration, and a key to successful creative developments yet to be achieved by designers.

# Chapter 16
## Design Matters

As a term, design refers to creative functionality where trained individuals implement certain skills to achieve desired results. Initially, design is divided into multiple disciplines which specialise in certain fields. Various sectors relate to design, though each branch deals with specific concerns. To users, consumers, and perceivers, design will always matter greatly. Whether such individuals notice the obvious significance of design or not, the initial purpose of designing will continue to impact people of all sorts. Design as a subject aims to influence people in many possible ways. By merging creativity with logic, design becomes maintained so opportunities facing designers will certainly be endless. Creatives develop solutions based on certain needs and necessities. Therefore, anything being produced by designers will have a desired intention. For graphic designers specifically, the aim is to produce visually communicative solutions which are creative in every aspect. For a field of such importance, creative solutions developed by creatives should happen to be effective in order to result as successful.

A graphic designer's role at this stage becomes different in a way compared with other design professions. Since for graphic designers especially, responsibility will be greater. Constantly generating ideas that cause creatives to develop effective creative solutions will be a key factor. Any solution developed by designers should have an impact on other individuals. Such a marked effect on others will reveal why design matters significantly. An influence on perceivers because of a creative solution reveals the link between communication and understanding.

Generally, people communicate to understand and acknowledge one another while gradually gaining awareness at the same time. Visual communication as an approach aims to spread awareness from informative solutions developed entirely by designers. Surely, creative abilities differ from one designer to another, though with passion there will always be room for improvement. Creatives who are willing to develop personal skills and understanding will be able to perform with confidence while being determined. Creative solutions developed by creatives with competent characteristics will be more likely to succeed whenever applied. Enlightened designers will be aware and informed of vital requirements a complete design requires in order to result as effective. Design as a subject aims to impact other individuals by having an effect on behaviour and performance. Basically, a designer's goal is to aid an individual's performance by producing effective outcomes which support function.

As a profession, design demands for a complex analysing system where creatives become in charge of developing effective solutions that continue to influence others. A creative system where designers generate ideas and implement certain skills to achieve results that matter to communities and societies. Outcomes which have been developed by designers are meant to influence perceivers to react in a specific way. Creatives originally begin a design process with a desired intention, without which a creative outcome would not result as an effective solution. A particular intention from designers will be the cause for commencing a design process, since a certain intention from creatives will be the reason behind developing an outcome that is meant to have an impact on others. Perceivers, users, and consumers all rely on visual communication to function freely. Such individuals depend on design immensely, because design will continue to be an essential part of anyone's life. Every individual should clearly admit and accept that design, as an approach matters to great extent. Undeniably, design should be regarded as a creative approach that links perceivers to understanding. An approach of such significance impacts people globally through various solutions which matter greatly and have been developed entirely by creatives.

Design as a subject is divided into multiple branches which all have creativity and innovation in common. However, the functionality of each branch differs from one another. Surely, design as an industry can be seen as an ever-evolving field, where the purpose of designing remains to serve people by developing creative needs based on certain requirements. Designers from various fields generally begin a design process with a cause that leads to creativity. For designers, it will always be necessary to identify such a cause prior to designing, since a desired intention gradually unfolds to aid designers throughout a creative process. Branches of design serve people based on certain needs. For instance, fashion design is related to garment designing. Any fashion designer will aim to develop ideas based on trends or seasons, which, in the end, satisfies a certain market. Just like fashion design, interior design also serves people by introducing ideas that relate to home décor and furnishing. People basically require services related to design in order to solve certain concerns or look for an appropriate solution.

Unlike other fields of design, graphic design specifically deals with solutions which require a greater responsibility because of having an influence on others. Graphic design has to do with the development of visually communicative solutions which should express creativity by all means. Anything graphic designers develop should convey a visual message which basically delivers meaning to perceivers. A field like graphic design deals with visual communication and the process of developing effective solutions. Transmitting meaningful communication with creative aspects to perceivers requires skill and understanding, since the success of any proposed idea depends entirely on a creative's reaction. Dealing with matters related to visual communication demands for enlightened creatives who are aware of knowledgeable facts and information. Graphic designers should be individuals who possess valuable and useful resources to back up any creative solution yet to be produced.

A perceiver's reaction will totally be a designer's concern, since the way in which a perceiver or consumer reacts, towards a creative solution gives designers a further understanding of behaviour. Creative individuals develop solutions to help people function. So, any affect a proposed creative solution has on perceivers will be credited to designers. Inevitably, a profession like design deserves much more recognition by people who rely on such an approach, since acknowledging the importance design portrays will support creatives massively by encouraging individuals to maintain creativity. All the multiple fields of design have concerns that relate to various issues and matters which require creativity to be solved. Designers are individuals who are trained and qualified to face demands related to the creative industry. By the application of certain skills, designers become able to achieve objectives without any complications.

Surely roles of designers may differ from one another, though the mission behind developing creative solutions will always remain the same. Design is known to be the solution for many matters concerning functionality. Therefore, as creatives, designers should always be prepared whenever required. Services related to the design industry will continue to be available, though it is up to designers to achieve requests and seek commissioning. As long as designers express proficient attributes, opportunities will continue to emerge. Designers who are active constantly are more likely to achieve successful outcomes. A profession like design surely demands a lot of effort from creatives, though without such insistence, design would not flourish. Creatives should represent the design industry efficiently at all times in order to gain successful outcomes regularly. Design should be considered a notable profession controlled by competent creatives.

Realizing that as a profession design will continue to have an influence of some sort on others will be essential for designers. Comparing design with other professions reveals the importance behind the actual purpose of designing. Surely most creatives dismiss the fact that creative productions are meant to have an impact on others. A designer's role is to generate creative yet imaginative ideas which evolve into effective outcomes. Usually, designers go through a creative process where ideas are transformed and developed into solutions. Such a development phase is extremely crucial for creatives. During a creative process, designers become in control of developing solutions which should result as effective towards a desired target. Without resources that act like supportive material, creatives would basically fail at achieving effective solutions. Implementing design fundamentals and principles would not be enough to achieve such solutions, which literally explains why design is dissimilar from other professions. What makes design unique is how unconventional such a subject happens to be. Design is not based on history, a certain set of rules, or particular opinions.

As an approach, design can be described as a resolution which offers endless opportunities and possibilities. Anyone willing to enter such a path should be prepared to constantly enhance understanding in order to succeed at a profession of such significance. Lacking understanding and knowledge will prevent creativity to develop. As designers, creatives should attempt developing personal understanding frequently. By becoming enlightened individuals, designers will gain confidence while developing proficient features a profession like design demands for. Enhancing personal attributes will allow designers to maintain creativity while gaining valuable experience. After all, designers who represent a profession like design should express dominant characteristics in order to attract attention, since individuals with influential characteristics will be more likely to have an effect on other individuals, which would cause others to inquire more about the creative industry.

Representing a profession requires appeal and interest, since the presence of an individual reflects specific features anyone might possess. So, the way in which an individual performs or acts may inspire any soul from anywhere. Such an effect will help the creative industry attract audiences who may someday be part of the design world. Realizing that a profession like design aims to affect others by having an influence on a character's behaviour will support creatives throughout any development process. By becoming aware of the purpose of designing, creatives will develop solutions more carefully, since any outcome yet to be produced should result as effective in order to be influential. Designers should aim to have some sort of influence towards a desired target at all times. By identifying a cause for developing a creative solution, designers will be prepared to develop creative solutions which are more likely set to have an effect on others. Overall, design as a profession combines creativity with logic for goals to be achieved. Designers create to have an effect on others, to inspire others, and most importantly to help people function.

Each and every field of design aims to have an impact on other souls. Whether creatives develop solutions or objects, anything intended from creatives will initially have the exact same goal. It is vital for creatives to keep in mind that the purpose of designing is to have an impact on others by serving creative yet meaningful needs. Any sort of influence on any other soul because of a creative solution will reveal how design can be influential. Designers should represent a profession like design in the best possible way, since appearance and presence will be essential towards opportunities facing designers. Engaged and active designers will continue to develop knowledgeable attributes which will greatly aid any design process yet to come. With practice, knowledge gradually develops into experience which for creatives will be crucial towards personal enhancement.

For a field like graphic design, solutions become the link between perceivers and understanding. Creative solutions developed by graphic designers should be visually communicative in order to depict a certain message, which explains why an approach like visual communication somehow integrates with graphic design. Surely, visual communication is regarded as an aspect of graphic design because of the significance such an approach expresses, since most of the solutions developed by graphic designers are concerned with visual communication. As a field, graphic design consists of principles related to visual communication which expresses why such an approach relates to graphic design most. Typography is considered a major design principle for graphic designers. Basically, the field of type and linguistic meaning is part of nearly anything a graphic designer intends on developing.

Expressing messages through visual forms supports communication that requires to be delivered towards a desired target. Perceivers distinguish informative solutions developed entirely by creatives. Anyone who underestimates the significance of design should question how perceivers would function without creative solutions? Taking a moment to realise that creative solutions do actually matter, and that designers in control of achieving such results are the force behind such effective solutions will reveal the influence design has on people of all sorts. Visual communication will continue to be seen as a successful approach as long as creatives activate effective ideas by developing results that have an impact on people. Generally, perceivers recognise information being directed towards them for a specific cause. Any sort of information visually expressed will aim to deliver a certain message to spread awareness. A perceiver may be any individual who perceives visual communication by discerning meaningful solutions which are expressive. Basically, any solution developed by a designer would have a desired intention prior to being revealed. So, by the time a solution is perceived, an intended target would have benefited from the overall outcome.

Creatives are commissioned to deliver visually attractive solutions which are meant to spread awareness. Surely any sort of awareness would have originally been from communicative elements a designer includes in a design to result as a meaningful solution. A matter of such reveals that creativity on its own would not attract viewers, though by incorporating logic and linguistics with creativity, meaning becomes expressed through visual solutions. Designers should be aware that meaning expressed from creative solutions should be clear and straight forward in order to have an effect on a desired target. Normally, creatives do not realise that perceivers differ from another. There can never be a creative solution that resolves a particular global matter. Since perceivers from around the world may function on a certain language which will only be common around a specific group of people. Creative solutions which deliver visually expressed communication can be available in multiple convenient forms as long as creatives prepare themselves to face such challenging tasks. Enticing a perceiver surely requires study and practice. Only by developing knowledge and researching well enough will creatives discover practical solutions. By studying a perceiver carefully, designers will discover various unconventional ways that will eventually be helpful.

Certainly, a field like graphic design demands a lot from creatives, though only with a vigorous amount of effort will designers ever succeed. Visual communication will be the link between perceivers and understanding as long as such an approach is applied. Over the years, visual communication has evolved immensely because of passionate creatives who have developed thinking abilities to achieve successful outcomes which shape the creative industry today. Perceivers from around the world rely on visual communication due to being a convenient approach that makes understanding accessible for everyone. Designers should keep developing skills and knowledge in order to be active individuals, while also looking for enhancements that might aid an industry like design someday.

Undeniably, design is known to be an effective approach towards many users, perceivers, or consumers. Design may be referred to as the solution to certain problems or an answer from a particular situation. Some might consider design as an approach while others may identify design as a method. No one can ever decide on a specific description that best describes design. Truly, a subject like design will always happen to be unpredictable because of the unlimited possibilities continuing to evolve. However, all designers agree that design is an effective approach because of being successful at having a desired effect on users. As creatives, designers generate ideas based on certain needs that cause creative solutions to unfold. Developing innovative outcomes with the intention of having an effect makes design an effective approach. Surely users do not realise that any creative solution has been developed with the intention of alluring and tempting viewers to act in a specific way. Creative solutions have been influencing perceivers and consumers ever since design was introduced centuries ago. A certain effect on behaviour or performance from a creative solution will be a designer's intention.

Creatives set objectives prior to designing; generally most objectives would aim to have some sort of influence on a desired target. Creatives will always face a challenging task whenever trying to achieve effective solutions, since the success of an outcome depends entirely on the reactions perceivers or consumers may have. Failing to achieve a successful response will prevent creatives from achieving effective solutions. Designers may experience failure at some stage eventually, though preparing for a reaction will strengthen a creative's mentality. Reacting in a positive way by accepting defeat to learn from such an experience will motivate creatives to achieve successful outcomes regularly.

With continuous practice, designers will be able to develop skills while gaining experience. For creatives, especially, experience matters greatly. It is with experience that designers manage to find a suitable solution that best serves people. Based on the experience levels each designer attains, outcomes become prominently affected. Therefore, creatives should always develop understanding in order to be enlightened. Design will continue to be the solution to many concerns, though at the same time design will continue to evolve because of an impact that remains active. Creative solutions may spread awareness or affect behaviour; in any case, a solution developed by creatives is meant to influence others. Designers basically develop practical solutions which should be functional, useful, or sensible. Surely, each field related to design operates in a certain way, though the purpose of designing will always be similar. Solutions developed by creatives are meant to aid functionality while being useful at the same time. For instance, solutions developed to direct people to certain places are aimed to affect drivers, travellers, or commuters. Such solutions should express clarity in order to be effective.

Certainly, it will be the designer's role to research more

about a desired target prior to developing a solution, since any solution yet to be achieved should be successful at producing a desired intention from creatives. An influential intention from creatives will be the cause of an effective solution that designers actually intend on producing. In this case, a designer will have to develop signs and symbols which express meaningful information to any viewer requiring assistance in direction. By perceiving such informative solutions, commuters begin to react in a certain way which has been influenced from a particular creative solution. Communication expressed visually has been effective and successful towards any certain perceiver. Surely designers become responsible for developing such effective solutions, since the process of producing such influential results requires skilled creatives with certain abilities.

Designers are trained individuals who express creative skills, though the process of designing would not be achievable with creativity on its own. Designers should realise that in order to impact others, logic should assist creativity for any sort of influence to occur. Designers as creatives should enable creativity while maintaining a certain level of knowledge. Without knowledgeable attributes, creatives will always find it difficult to generate ideas which originally support an effective solution. Maintaining creativity will be extremely vital for creatives at any stage of their career. Developing understanding by enlightening one's soul opens up many possibilities. Especially as designers, creatives who obtain knowledge from multiple sources will be more likely to exceed at a profession like design. With understanding, experience gradually develops, and for designers there will never be enough experience to retain. Creatives will always be judged based on experience, since the level of experience a designer possesses reveals a person's capabilities. In an industry like design, experience portrays professionalism and competence. Leaving a fine impression towards others will surely be rewarding for creatives.

A creative approach like design spreads awareness to anyone seeking understanding. Surely design can solve various issues anyone can ever imagine, though the overall intention for designing is to spread awareness towards a desired target. Basically, the perception of creative solutions enlightens perceivers in specific ways. Anyone facing or using a creative solution will eventually gain a certain message which has been initially intended. Consumers as well are known to consume products based on desire and preference, which have been originally intended to satisfy a certain market. Awareness from such solutions reveal that creative developments are able to inform perceivers in certain ways while gaining consciousness. Design as a matter will continue to support awareness as long as creatives generate effective solutions which are meant to convey meaningful information. By influencing perceivers, creatives become in control of the performance and behaviour that such individuals might retain. Even thinking may be affected from creative solutions, since some solutions are aimed to affect decisions yet to be made by perceivers or users.

Consciousness is the state of being aware of one's surrounding. Creative solutions developed by creatives are meant to direct people while aiding functionality. Also, creative solutions assist people to achieve certain needs. As an approach, design will have the ability to affect others while raising awareness. Such an effect on perceivers displays the significance design has on people of all sorts. Thinking of perceivers makes someone want to investigate even further to who exactly belongs to such a word. Inquiring about a matter of such relevance or consequence is not considered as a negative approach. Instead, becoming aware of undisclosed matters which have been disregarded by many will somehow enlighten any individual immensely. A perceiver is basically anyone who discerns or recognises informative solutions in order to gain consciousness. Perceivers may distinguish various solutions which portray visual messages. As an approach, visual communication happens to support the way in which perceivers function. Anything perceived visually by people of various backgrounds delivers some sort of message which helps with gaining awareness.

Creative solutions which support visual communication aim to ease perception while delivering meaningful messages. Perceivers may be regarded as individuals who seek information in order to function. Surely each and every perceiver will eventually benefit in a certain way, since requirements may differ from one perceiver to another. However, the overall intention of developing such effective solutions will be to gain awareness. Creative solutions developed by designers will continue to have different intentions depending on certain requirements, since designers are meant to develop effective solutions based on certain needs. Achieving objectives will be a tough challenge facing any designer, surely, though accomplishing any planned objective will reveal how outcomes matter greatly towards desired targets. Anything a designer intends on producing should have some sort of effect on perceivers, users, or consumers.

Depending on who exactly the target happens to be, creatives will be able to develop a suitable solution. Identifying a specific target group prior to designing will be crucial for creatives, since any proposed plan would aim to satisfy a certain group of people. By researching in depth about an expected target, creatives will be able to develop solutions instantly without any complications. Understanding the cause for designing will lead designers directly to effective solutions.

Once creatives become aware of a reason, intentions will gradually unfold and so objectives become identified. A design process is considered a crucial stage for creatives, since not only are solutions developed during such a phase, aims are also meant to be accomplished as well. Creative yet effective solutions developed by creatives depend on a successful process where ideas are evolved into final outcomes. Design will continue to matter greatly towards various classifications of people because of requirements that commence a design process. Combining creativity with logic aids understanding while prompting consciousness.

Mainly, design should be seen as an approach that connects people to raise personal awareness. Considering design as a vital matter will support such a profession to flourish even further. As designers, creatives should represent a field like design with competent attributes in order to leave a pleasing impression. Designers are the force behind creative solutions; individuals with such creative abilities should be more confident and self-assured. Revealing such attributes will express true qualities designers should obtain. Creatives who control a field like design should also be aware of the responsibility facing each designer. It will be the designer's duty fully to develop effective solutions constantly in order to achieve any success. Failing to accomplish effective solutions will prevent designers from gaining recognition. Creatives should be acknowledged because of the impact such effective solutions have on multiple communities. Continuing to develop solutions and outcomes which aim to influence people will be necessary for designers who wish to be recognised.

Design as a subject has always aimed at having an impact on others. An influence of such sense can be noticed on anyone being in contact with anything related to design. Surely design as a term relates to many concerns an individual might have, since as a broad subject, design will remain unlimited and never restricted to certain matters. An identification of such breadth will make anyone realise that a subject like design should be recognised because of the significance it expresses. Many communities and societies have been affected by matters related to design. Developments and productions created by designers have influenced many souls while making a statement. Design matters greatly because of the impact it has on people's behaviour and understanding. There will be multiple moments or incidents in which design becomes identified as an influential approach. Reactions will judge and reveal the effect creative solutions have on individuals from various backgrounds.

Visual communication as an approach leads, directs, and guides individuals to achieve personal needs. While design remains active, awareness will continue to spread. Everyone requires consciousness in order to understand and function. Design offers awareness from effective creative solutions which are meant to have an impact on souls. Acknowledging a matter like design will reward designers with countless opportunities. A practice like design should be considered a significant field where creativity collides with logic to impact others. As creatives, designers should always be aware of the initial aim a design proposes. With informative sources and facts, skills are gradually enhanced. As creatives, constant development will be required for any successful achievement.